WHAT PEOPLE ARE SAYING ABOUT
MindWalks:

"A truly peaceful book and companion to life."

> DR. RICHARD CARLSON
> Author
> *Don't Sweat the Small Stuff ... and It's All Small Stuff*

"*MindWalks* is a wonderful guide to the joys,
delights, and peace to be discovered in walking ...
Thoreau once remarked that he knew of only a few
who understood the art of walking. I think that had
he read *MindWalks*, Thoreau would have added
Mary Frakes to his short list."

> LANE CONN, PH.D
> The Center for Psychology and Social Change

"Anyone who is overwhelmed by the demands of
modern life should buy this book. *MindWalks* is
a great way to destress."

> CHUCK MARTIN
> Author
> *Net Future*

D0683922

MindWalks

100 Easy Ways
to Relieve Stress, Stay Motivated,
and Nourish Your Soul

Mary H. Frakes

Life Lessons
Cambridge, Massachusetts

MINDWALKS™ is a trademark owned by Mary H. Frakes.

Permissions information appears after the acknowledgments.

Printed in Canada.

Publisher's Cataloging-in-Publication Data
(Provided by Quality Books, Inc.)

Frakes, Mary H.
    MindWalks: 100 easy ways to relieve stress, stay
motivated, and nourish your soul / Mary H. Frakes.
    — 1st ed.
      p. cm.
    Includes bibliographical references.
    LCCN: 98-96770
    ISBN: 0-9667879-4-3

    1. Walking-Psychological aspects. 2. Stress management.
3. Meditations. 4. Self-actualization (Psychology) I. Title.

RA 781.65.F73 1999   613.7'176
                                  QBI98-1575

Edition:
10 9 8 7 6 5 4 3 2 1

TABLE OF CONTENTS

Thinking Things Through 61

Managing Stress 81

Acknowledgments

Thanks to Mary Allen, Dominique Callimanopoulos, Dr. John F. Hamsher, Rebecca Martin, Carol Page, Jan Swafford, and Joan Weston, who were kind enough to review early versions of *MindWalks* and make suggestions that improved the book immensely. For years, each in his or her own way has taught me many valuable life lessons. Casey Meyers helped me make sure that my suggestions don't present physical problems for MindWalkers.

Cynthia Rose cleaned up the words, and John Miller and Aaron Kenedi of Big Fish Design made the cover as inspiring and elegant as I had hoped. Josh Faigen of Full Circle Type in Pittsburgh deserves special thanks for saving me from hubris in print.

Chuck Martin first taught me about the power of optimism and determination and encouraged me to trust my instincts. I am blessed by his friendship.

And finally, my heartfelt thanks to my parents, Margaret and John Hamsher. Their support, love, and encouragement through the years, even when they may have privately doubted my sanity, have meant more than they know.

Introduction

I once read a quotation from artist Bruce Nauman: "An awareness of yourself comes from a certain amount of activity." It stuck with me, perhaps because it expressed so perfectly the reason I began taking MindWalks several years ago.

What is a MindWalk, you ask? A MindWalk is as much about inspiration as perspiration. It helps you achieve the mental and spiritual benefits of walking. If you're already a walker, MindWalks can bring variety to your route; if you're just starting, they can help motivate you to stick with it. They can be done at a fast pace or slowly; in the city, country, or suburbs; on a long walk or short one; alone or with a companion.

Scientific studies have shown time and again that walking provides many of the health benefits of running, without the stress on joints. There are many excellent books that can help you understand walking as physical exercise. They prescribe regimens, teach proper form, and help you monitor your pace so you're getting the best possible cardiovascular workout. In the Appendix, I've provided a list of resources that can help you develop a structured exercise program.

MindWalks is not designed to replace exercise books. I simply want to help your mind benefit from your walks as much as your body does. If you enjoy your walks more, you're more likely to make them a regular part of your day. People who abandon exercise programs often report that they gave up because they just plain got bored. When you're MindWalking, every walk becomes an exploration, an opportunity for magic. A MindWalk can help you:

• Enjoy the beauty of the world around you
• Think through problems
• Motivate yourself to pursue and succeed at your goals
• Manage your emotions
• Reduce stress
• Be more comfortable with your body
• Awaken your creativity

I developed the concept of MindWalks at a time when I felt as though the world had chewed me up and spit me out. Career demands had left me little time for a personal life—and then even my professional life fell apart. For several months, I did little besides try to get through the day at work, come home, eat whatever hadn't gone bad, and collapse. In full retreat from the world, I became expert at escaping reality by thumbing a ride on the remote control.

When spring came, I began walking—and healing. As I struggled to get rid of depression flab, I began to sort out what had happened to me and why. The energy generated by simply putting one foot in front of the other buffered the pain enough that I could begin to examine it, to hold it for a while without flinching. Walking seemed to help me fight internal battles that I had been trying to flee by immersing myself in reruns and TV cooking shows. The rhythm of my feet replaced the drone of angry self-criticism in my brain. In some inexplicable way, the path returned me to myself.

I began to realize that every MindWalk, as I had begun to call them, held at least one thing—a sight, a sound, a new discovery—that made getting outdoors worthwhile (see "There's Always Something"). Once I came to expect and look for them, these small events began to change how I looked at the world. No matter what happened during the day, I could remember the one brief moment of beauty I had carved out for myself. Wondering what that day's walk would present helped motivate me to get out and walk on days when I felt like staying in bed. Walking gave my mind the time and space it needed to work out problems and come to terms with whatever was disturbing my soul. And the weight lost by walking every day made me feel more comfortable in my skin.

This book is organized into nine sections, each of which highlights a different aspect of MindWalking. Some, such as "Reconnecting with Your Body," are more instructional; others, such as "MindWalks in Time and Place," are meditations that may help you experience more fully the beauty of a particular season, time of day, or place. The sections are designed to be sampled at will. You'll probably find that you respond to some MindWalks more than others, but I hope you'll at least explore each of the sections, however briefly. Each can open your eyes to new ways to enrich your life.

I hope MindWalks will inspire you to make your own discoveries, to find new joy in the world around you, and to use your walks as a time for reflection and meditation. Walk for exercise to nourish the body—and MindWalk to nourish your soul.

ONE SPECIAL THING EACH DAY

Let your ears hear whatever they want to hear; let your eyes see whatever they want to see; let your mind think whatever it wants to think; let your lungs breathe in their own rhythm.

ALAN WATTS

There's Always Something

I began doing MindWalks to get in shape. Consistency in working out had never been my strong point, and walking was no exception; in the mornings, I often looked for any excuse to stay in bed and avoid exercise. But after a month or so I realized that every time I managed to get out, I had at least one experience during my walk that made me glad I had put on my shoes.

Sometimes it was a gorgeous view I had never noticed. Sometimes it was two colors that intensified each other in a particular light, the way a robin's-egg sky enriches the yellow of backlit sunflowers. Sometimes it was the first daffodil of the year, or the scent of lilacs by a fence, or a clean, crisp bird's feather. I learned to anticipate that day's discovery, to watch for things I would not have seen otherwise. That anticipation became the motivator for my whole walking program, a game I played with myself. It's been several years now since I began expecting one special thing from each walk; not once have I failed to find it.

MindWalks are about discovery. Even if your route never varies, becoming truly aware of your surroundings turns every venture outdoors into an exploration.

Seasons rotate, bringing with them new foliage that buds out, then blooms, then fades as you check on it every day. The weather changes its mind; the sun rises at a slightly different time and alters how the light hits everything you see. The same old stuff? Only if you don't pay attention.

One of my favorite MindWalk moments came one day when I was resting on a bench, gazing across a river bordered by a jogging trail. I idly watched as a young girl came jogging down the path in front of me, her hair slicked back into a ponytail. Not an unusual sight— except for the parakeet perched atop her head like a hood ornament.

This was clearly a routine for both of them; just as they crossed in front of me, he hopped down to cling to her ponytail as if it were a branch. On they jogged, the bird bob-bob-bobbing along with her every stride. It became an unforgettable mental snapshot.

Granted, you're not going to see a hitchhiking parakeet every day. But looking for something special on each walk becomes a self-fulfilling prophecy. If you resolve to find one experience each day that makes you glad you got outdoors, I guarantee you won't be disappointed.

Walk with Freud

Freud had a very simple explanation for students who asked him how to practice his psychological precepts. He told them it was simple: "Look! Listen!" Freud's simple advice also applies to a MindWalk. All that is required to make each excursion outdoors something more than exercise is to be acutely aware of our surroundings.

How often do we really look at what is going on around us? What we observe and experience on a walking route can be as beneficial for the soul as the walking is for the body. We are so surrounded by artificial objects, so assaulted by all forms of secondhand experience, so inundated with demands from daily life, that we forget what it is like to let our senses take over and inspire our minds.

Take a few moments at some point during each walk to become thoroughly engaged with something. Layer a small fan-shaped gingko leaf on top of a larger one and look at the exquisite pattern that results. Take the time to closely examine and touch a natural object; even bits of gravel, looked at closely, can reveal striking patterns, colors, or textures. When you smell a flowering vine along your route, inhale the scent deeply to coat your lungs with its perfume. Watching a chipmunk or squirrel for a few minutes can reveal its unique animal personality.

Luxuriate in these moments of profound awareness, these fleeting pleasures as private as a thought. They are tiny, transient works of performance art created and discovered by you alone—treasures that cost nothing.

Look! Listen!

See with New Eyes

Unless we travel to do our walking, we often wind up retracing the same routes over and over again. How then can we find new things to delight us?

The secret is in how we look.

In her inspiring book, *Drawing On the Right Side of the Brain*, Betty Edwards discusses two different ways in which the brain processes information. The first is the mode in which we usually operate: linear, logical, verbal. We look at something and see an object: A flower is a sweet-smelling plant, a building is a structure, a stone is a mineral formation. An object is defined by its function, by our experience of it in the past, and by the name we apply to it.

The second way in which the brain processes information is intuitive rather than logical, holistic rather than linear, visual instead of verbal. When this mode is dominant—and activating it often requires conscious effort—we look at something and see only what is actually in front of our eyes, instead of being distracted by the symbolic associations that our logic-dominated brains have built up around it. A flower is perceived not as the object called "flower" but as a pattern created by its petals. A building is a collection of angles and lines and textures; a rain-washed stone becomes a palette blended from neutral tones.

The reason we're sometimes surprised by what we see in a photo we've taken is because we're operating in the first mode, our brains focusing on what we're photographing and filtering out the rest ("I'm taking a picture of Fred in front of the Washington Monument"). However, the camera operates in the second, recording exactly what's there ("Here's Fred with the Washington Monument sticking out of his head").

Artists train themselves to use the second mode. It becomes second nature to them to see not the flower but its form, not an object but its color or position relative to other objects. These other aspects of seeing are the basis of abstract paintings that have no subject but are simply about the richness of the colors in them or the way lines are arranged.

As you walk, try seeing the world as a painter might. Even in surroundings that have little natural beauty, learning to see without thinking about what you're looking at can help you discover beauty in unexpected places. Look at patterns or colors rather than things. Find beauty in the accidental compositions that nature creates, in much the same way as Picasso did when he dashed off quick sketches in a café. You may be struck by a grouping of leaves, or the vertical stripes of light through a picket fence. Learn to separate color from what it is on; the homeliest objects can display exquisite coloration.

Unless doing so endangers your ability to walk safely, try taking off your glasses to enhance your ability to see shape and pattern and color rather than objects. Some artists deliberately unfocus their eyes (think of looking at those 3-D images concealed in flat printed patterns) to create new perceptions of the world around them. They call it "seeing with soft eyes." As you walk, train yourself to see with new eyes.

Raise Your Line of Sight

Discovering your surroundings can be difficult if your eyes are glued to the ground directly in front of your feet, as mine too often are. The sidewalks where I do most of my walking are partly to blame; they tend to be uneven and treacherous for an unwary foot. Staring mindlessly at the ground is a habit that's too easy to fall into, even on smoother terrain free of protruding tree roots and canine land mines. But walking along looking only two feet ahead isn't good for your walking posture, and it certainly isn't good for the spirit. It's hard for your soul to soar if your attention is anchored to the pavement.

Here's my solution, which I came to after someone told me how to cut a straight line with a pair of scissors. The trick is looking not at where the scissors are actually cutting, but at a point a few inches ahead of the blades. Try it yourself; you'll be amazed at how much truer the cut is.

As you walk, try picking a spot twenty to thirty yards in front of you. Quickly scan the path ahead up to that point for hazards—potholes, stray branches, dog poop, whatever. Register their approximate locations and then relax. Once you know where the potential hazards are and roughly when you'll need to avoid them, you can look down when you need to without worrying about tripping or stepping in something.

Once you reach your selected point, pick a new spot ahead and again scan the path up to it (the scan should take no more than a couple of steps). Raising your horizons regularly frees you to look around more, to notice the details that make your walk an exploration. This may take some practice, but it will soon become as automatic as looking at the ground in front of you used to be, and your walks will be richer for the small wonders you're now able to see.

Think for a minute about what this implies for how we approach our daily lives. If you go through the days looking down, focusing only on the obstacles and poop that life serves up regularly, that's all you're going to see. I'm not suggesting that you ignore the possible hazards, just that you remind yourself to raise your line of sight. You need to keep looking down the path toward your goal and revel in your surroundings if you're going to enjoy the journey.

Lift your eyes and lift your soul.

Outdoor Magic

The art of magic lies in the revelation of the unexpected. If rabbits came packaged with the sale of every hat, we wouldn't be surprised when the magician reaches in and pulls out a pair of long ears. Part of the joy of walking also lies in being presented with surprises. But to find those unanticipated gifts, we must look at the world with eyes wide open and a spirit attuned to miraculous detail.

There's a wonderful book by John R. Stilgoe, a professor of landscape history at Harvard University. The book, called *Outside Lies Magic*, shows how much we can learn about human history by really looking at the world around us instead of bustling blindly through life.

Stilgoe's Harvard course teaches what he calls "the art of exploration." He studies the impact of people by focusing on small, observed details of what he calls the "shaped land." His students of the last twenty years still write to him about the small discoveries they've made because of the skills he taught them: the ways that children's playground equipment has changed over the decades, the different colors of the raincoats worn by eastbound and westbound passengers at Chicago's

O'Hare Airport, the pattern of limestone erosion on New York City streets.

I love Stilgoe's initial directive: "Go outside, move deliberately, then relax, slow down, look around. Do not jog. Do not run. Forget about blood pressure and arthritis, cardiovascular rejuvenation, and weight reduction. Instead, pay attention to everything that abuts the rural road, the city street, the suburban boulevard. Walk. Stroll. Saunter. Ride a bike and coast a lot. Explore."

Magic, says Stilgoe, is to be found almost anywhere but at eye level. So when you go for your MindWalk today, look up. Look down. Look closely. Look for the unexpected magic.

If you look closely enough, you'll find it.

See with Touch

For all of us, there are days when we feel as though we're simply adrift in the universe. Meaning and purpose seem to elude us. We seem to be going nowhere, leaving nothing by which to be remembered. Gray colors our souls, and we move dully from task to task, trying to remember why we're going through the motions. We need to be reminded of our own value.

On days like this, try a MindWalk based on an exercise suggested by Dr. Michael Cohen, whose book *Reconnecting with Nature* reminds us how much we lose by cutting ourselves off from the natural environment. You'll need only a felt-tipped pen, plus pockets in whatever you're wearing.

At the beginning of your walk, select a half-dozen pebbles that are as identical as you can find. If you're on the beach you can use small shells; in the woods, acorns or tiny pine cones can substitute. The key to this exercise is that all of your selections be as alike in size and shape as possible. Mark one with your pen, and put the others in a convenient pocket. As you walk, concentrate on getting to know the stone you marked, using only your sense of touch. Feel the way one end curves a little more sharply than another. Let your fingertips become aware of the beginning of a crack on one side, a tiny bump at its bottom—things you probably didn't see when you were trying to match six identical stones. Take your time: five to ten minutes is about right.

Then put it into your pocket with the others and mix them up, taking care not to keep track of which is the marked stone. When the pebble is thoroughly lost among the rest, see if you can sort through your pocket —again, without looking—to find the marked stone by touch alone. You'll find that each one, seemingly so like the others when you picked it out, has its own unique form and markings. Says Cohen, "This activity helps bring into our consciousness the diverse uniqueness found in every aspect of nature, along with an awareness of our lack of sensitivity to the ability of nature, within and around us, to create harmony from diversity."

Discovery of what's special in anything requires only our careful attention. Let each stone teach you something about your own uniqueness in the world—even if that world seems to think you're just another pebble.

The Big Picture

"When you take a flower in your hand and really look at it, it's your world for the moment." So said Georgia O'Keeffe, whose paintings show that she was a master of MindWalks through her beloved New Mexico hills.

O'Keeffe loved to paint something as small as a poppy on an area big enough to fill a wall. Somehow the flower seems larger than the canvas it's on; it absorbs the space around it. The artist's intense concentration, her immersion in its color and form, gives profound impact to every detail of what to the rest of the world is just a simple flower.

We hear a lot about how important it is to focus on the big picture. Sometimes, though, I think that we don't focus enough on the small, the obscure, the neglected detail that can help bring the big picture into better focus. O'Keeffe wanted to paint flowers large because she knew that otherwise people would not really see them. Their brains would automatically register "flower" and never get beyond that named concept to the richness of color, the dramatic lines, the subtlety of fold and texture that she saw.

On your MindWalk today, take a moment to find a flower somewhere along your route and deliberately concentrate on it. Look at it closely, as if you have to describe it to someone else later. Bring it close to your face so you can see every little detail. Forget that this object is a flower and focus only on the patterns within the blossom, the delicate shadings of color, the scent. Let nothing else exist for you except what you see in your hand.

For the moment, let this simple flower become your world.

Read the Signs

Street signs can be both poetry and comedy. One of the delights of walking in an urban environment is the opportunity to look up and discover a quirky display of unintended humor.

For years, a firm near where I live got a lot of mileage from proudly putting its name on the sign out front: Long Funeral Services. On another street stands the Atomic Supermarket: An artifact of the era of black-and-white TVs and bomb shelters, does it now sell irradiated food? The window of a butcher's small shop displays an odd combination of bloodthirstiness and bouncy good cheer: "Live Poultry Fresh Killed!" A bar's facade sports three or four different names, reminders of previous layers of ownership that linger on like old customers after last call. Sadly, gone is the sign for Morey's jewelry store: "Home of great bargains—and Morey!"

A friend recalls seeing a sign in his hometown years ago that both greeted a church gathering and promoted the menu's daily special: "Welcome Church of God Liver and Onions." In Branson, Missouri, a hotel sign I saw announced its reopening and advertised for staff by proclaiming:

NEWLY RENOVATED
WAITRESSES WANTED

As you walk, keep an eye out for such little gems.
Who says the universe doesn't have a sense of humor?

Touch Therapy

When you look for the one thing that will make today's MindWalk special, it's easy to find sights, sounds, and smells. When a delicious lasagna is being cooked in one of the houses you pass, the scent is impossible to ignore. You can't help looking around you as you walk. And a scrap of conversation overheard or the sound of a radio playing the song you used to dance to in high school finds you without your having to seek it out.

Touch as a tool for experiencing the world requires a bit more effort. Touch is like the shy sister of the other senses: It requires nurturing and careful attention before it will reward you with its own connection to beauty. But with a bit of coaxing, it can enhance your walk as much as the others.

As you walk today, feel the smooth granite of a column, the soft fuzz on a sage leaf or an apricot at the market. Brush your hand over the top of a clipped spruce hedge to feel the soft green sprouts emerging from its even surface like tiny hairs. The silkiness of a pansy petal brushed against your face is like butterfly wings. The world is full of textures waiting to be explored.

And as you touch them, let them touch your heart.

One Square Foot of the Universe

I once laughed at a friend of mine when he told me he had spent an hour out in the woods watching ants. I thought to myself, "This is a man who not only has too much free time but who might end up deciding to pledge allegiance to their queen." And yet if I'm sitting on the ground, I, too, sometimes watch ants as they march about their business. These small soldiers' affairs are just as important to them as if they were played on a world stage.

As an exercise in concentration, take a moment during your walk to stop and really look at one square foot of ground. Select a patch free of asphalt or gravel, and see how many things have made this small area their home. Are there ants or worms? Are there ordinary rocks that glint with tiny flecks of mica? Look for infant blades of grass sprouting, much as wispy hairs do from a balding man's head. Nuts may have dropped from nearby trees; seeds may have been blown there on the wind. There is life there with its own rhythms, its own purpose that doesn't require our attention to have a reason for being.

Sometimes our lives seem to close in around us;

wherever we turn, we bump into bad luck or the results of bad decisions. Perhaps you haven't accomplished what you had hoped. Maybe a relationship has ended, a job eliminated by downsizing. You feel trapped, unimportant, anonymous. As you concentrate on your chosen patch of ground, think of it as a metaphor for everyday life, which teems with activity unnoticed by the rest of the world.

And as you walk on, remember that no matter how narrow our range, how restricted our circumstances, there are small miracles waiting to be discovered in whatever square foot of the universe we claim as ours.

Listen to Shapes

I have a composer friend whose ear for sound is precise and delicate. Background noises that barely register with others—the music in restaurants, for example—drive him crazy. He is constantly plinking and pinging and thunking things to see what they sound like (the first time he came over for dinner, I opened my front door to find him experimentally tapping out a rhythm on a metal stair rail). He is simply more attuned to the world's natural symphony than most people.

I asked him once how he creates his music. Does he hear melodies, or is the process more methodical, the result of following logical rules of composition? He thought a moment, then replied, "I hear shapes of sounds; they're sort of like clouds. You have to develop a language and structure for a piece, but first I hear the shapes."

Sound is the victim of its own ubiquity. We are surrounded by so much noise that to survive its constant presence, we force it into the background and overlay it with the things we see. Sudden outbursts get our attention—the nasal blat of a car horn, a jackhammer's steely staccato—but most of the time sound is buried beneath our consciousness. MindWalks can help us learn to coax it out.

At the beginning of a walk, take a moment to shut your eyes and concentrate on simply absorbing sounds. Tune your ears so you hear not only the obvious melodies but the underlying chords: the whoop of an ambulance in the distance, the plane humming overhead, the scritching of insects, the quietly sinister buzz of an electrical connection box, the lonely keening of a distant train whistle. Suddenly you are part of your surroundings in a different way. The borders between self and surroundings blur, and the corner of our brains that secretly refuses to believe in the existence of the rest of the world marvels.

As you walk, the sound shapes change. You wade through them, the sounds closing behind you like water. A brief gust of rock music blows from a radio just inside an open window. An air conditioner hums, keeping the family inside safe from sweltering heat. Beep, beep, beep … somewhere a truck is backing up; why? Even in a city, you can construct a whole refrain from bird sounds; scraps of passing conversations are opening lines for dramas that will unfold without you. In the country, insects buzz about your passing, like gossips at a party.

Listen to the world, and connect.

Walk at the World's Pace

All right, you say. I'm alert. I'm looking around, observing carefully, and waiting for the appearance of that MindWalk moment that will make my walk worthwhile. And nothing's happening.

Relax. There are days when the world just seems to be an endless stretch of ho-hum. Your mind has crawled into a cave somewhere and stuck a sign out front that says, "Hibernation in progress!" You may be tired or numbed by sorrow. Or maybe there's nothing wrong, but you just can't seem to get yourself in a mindful state that's tuned in to your surroundings.

Maybe you're trying too hard. Don't feel as though you have to strain after insights as if you were a dog on a tight leash; that kind of pressure makes insight even more difficult to achieve. After all, a walk that simply gets you outdoors and moving isn't exactly a loss. At a minimum, you'll be physically energized, more prepared to make the most of whatever you might stumble upon later.

Turn off your anxious brain and simply focus on your bodily sensations: the sun (or rain) on your skin, the movement of your muscles, your breathing. The point of a MindWalk is to let your mind unfold to the world, like a flower opening to take in the sun, so it can be receptive to whatever the world has to offer. Paradoxically, you're most aware when your mind is most at rest.

Simply absorb instead of judging. Wait until the end of your walk, then try thinking back over everything you saw or heard or felt. If nothing special presents itself, choose one thing—even if it's a totally arbitrary choice—and decide that it has made your walk worth taking. I find that when I deliberately claim something as special, I automatically seem to discover ways in which it really *is* special.

And try walking a little longer. This may be one of those days when the brain takes longer to jump-start. In those few extra minutes, you may come across something totally unexpected. Trust the world to offer up something precious—at its own pace.

Believing Is Seeing

Eons of evolution notwithstanding, the brain can actually be pretty dumb. If we consciously lay down a certain pattern for the mind, it has a tendency to blithely follow that track. To demonstrate this to yourself, try thinking of a lemon. Imagine it clearly enough, and your mouth will begin to pucker; your brain has told your body to produce a physical reaction to a stimulus that exists only in your head. One study has shown that patients' bodies manufactured disease-resistant cells when the patients repeatedly visualized healthy cells as sharks swimming through their bloodstream, devouring the diseased ones.

The more you can imagine something occurring, the more likely you are to behave in ways that tend to make it happen. That's what makes visualization so important in achieving a goal; the dumb brain is following patterns laid down by repetition, consciously or unconsciously.

Walking is a perfect place to use visualization techniques; many of the mental exercises in this book rely on visualization for their effect. Walking tends to unleash the mind, even if you're going at a pretty good clip, and your brain is more receptive to being imprinted with

31

whatever images you choose to feed it during your walk.

On today's walk, visualize something you want to occur. The more detail you can put into your vision, the better. The image will begin to suggest steps you can take to help bring about the desired end. For example, if you visualize a spouse agreeing to help more around the house, you might also imagine new ways of getting that help. If you're trying to lose weight, visualize a thinner, fitter you striding along. I can practically guarantee you'll find yourself holding your body a little taller and walking at a more energetic pace.

Program your mind for possibility.

Reconnecting
with your
body

The mental pleasure in walking, as such, is in the sense
of power over all our moving machinery.

OLIVER WENDELL HOLMES

Sense Your Own Strength

If walking is part of a daily exercise routine for you, you'll inevitably build a layer of muscle. You can sense a certain firmness in your legs, your stomach, your back, that might not have been there before. Little by little, you begin to feel your own strength as you move, those muscles working with one another in concert. Even the inevitable small aches remind you that you are getting stronger. You find yourself unconsciously moving faster, almost bouncing with the joy of motion.

This awareness of your body's developing power can have a corresponding effect on your psychological well-being. Take pride in what you've done to get to this point. You've demonstrated the discipline it takes to improve your body. That strength of will is a resource you can use in other areas of your life. As your muscles work to keep you going, mentally translate that effort into a force you can direct against anything that may be bothering you. Think of your body as a weapon; punch the air like a boxer in training if you feel like it. Your strength is a new ally.

What if you're recuperating from a recent injury or suffering from chronic pain, if your doctor says you're able to move but you feel like a broken machine? Envision the blood flowing to the place that hurts, helping to wash away the ache and stiffness. Besides loosening up sore muscles, exercise stimulates the body to produce its own natural pain-killing chemicals, which can help tease your brain out of focusing on the parts that hurt. Even a few days spent suffering with a bad back underscores what a privilege free movement is once you're vertical again. As you walk more and more easily, revel in the sensation of being able to work your body, instead of taking motion for granted as we usually do.

Make friends with the strong, disciplined person who's emerging inside you.

Inner Stretching

Winter for me sometimes feels like an out-of-body experience. I know my physical being is in there somewhere underneath layer upon layer upon layer of clothing, but I feel detached from it. A hibernating animal, it is out of sight, out of mind. Warm weather brings me back from my disembodied state. Muscles seem to reattach themselves to nerve endings, and I stretch luxuriously inside my skin.

A good stretch that wakes us from cramped, dull torpor is a similar return to the body. We've all heard the warnings: Stretch before you exercise—even before a walk—to help prevent injury. But stretching also can be an opportunity to reinhabit your physical self. Most of the time, the brain arrogantly dominates the rest of our being; unless the body complains via ache or illness, it often gets ignored.

Any exercise book can teach you the proper technique for stretching. The main muscles to focus on are the hamstrings in the backs of the legs, the quadriceps on the front of the thighs, and the calf muscles. Think slow, gentle movements, not bounces. And just as you get your muscles ready to be exercised, you also can use your pre-workout stretch to prepare the mind for a MindWalk.

Focus on counting slowly as those muscles lengthen. Empty your mind of everything but the sensations in your legs, back, arms, and torso. Enjoy the sense of relief when you release the tension on the now-loosened muscles; it's a physical reminder of the mental relief you'll get with your MindWalk.

Use your stretches as a way to create a break between the daily hassles you're leaving behind temporarily and the renewing experience of a MindWalk. Awareness of your body while stretching readies your brain to experience your walk more deeply, to see things more fully. It helps your senses achieve equal status with your thoughts, enabling you to more fully absorb your surroundings.

As you're getting ready to walk today, try both outer and inner stretching. Your body and your mind will thank you.

The Mental Oil Change

You know the feeling. There's a knot in the pit of your stomach, your heart is racing, your muscles feel as tight as piano wire. Stress, fear, anger—any of these can cause adrenaline to start pumping through the body, creating the physical distress signs of a cornered animal.

Controlling your breathing can help you deal with these manifestations of high emotion. Our entire body responds to what our lungs are doing, even if we're not aware of it. The pace at which we take air in and let it out affects the functioning of our brain, our muscles, and our heart. Conscious breathing is a fundamental technique of meditation. It helps draw our attention away from external stimuli and the nagging voice in our heads, and places our awareness in the present moment.

Breathing meditations generally mean focusing on long, slow, regular breaths. However, an alternative technique can also help deal with stress, and it's easy to do when walking. Try a few of what I call "mental oil changes."

First, exhale sharply and quickly. Really push the air out of your lungs; let it come from your chest, your diaphragm, your shoulders, your spine. Think of trying to force out in one great gust of air all the stress and the negative emotions that clamor inside you.

Having cleared out some soul-smog, you can now fill that space with something fresh. Pull the new breath inward, inhaling deeply and much more slowly than you exhaled. Feel it gently filling you like a balloon, replacing the nasty gray gunk with untainted air and a calmer spirit. You may want to do this two or three times, to make sure you've really thoroughly recycled the air—and the stress reactions—in your body. (Don't overdo it, though; you don't want to hyperventilate or become light-headed.)

Think of this as a quick oil change for the mind and body. It won't solve any problems, but it can help calm you down quickly, leaving you refreshed and better able to cope with a stressful situation.

Pick Up the Pace

Sometimes we want a nice contemplative walk, in which we simply soak up our surroundings. Other times, though, it's good to get the heart going. We're not necessarily talking about racewalking, with its gliding hips and vigorous arms; studies have shown that walking at even a moderate pace can improve circulation, reduce stress, and lift mood. But you might be surprised at how invigorating a walk can be if you simply focus on walking a tiny bit faster. (If your heart is dicey, check with your doctor before trying this.)

There are two ways to do this: You can take longer or more frequent steps. For most people, taking slightly faster steps is much easier than learning racewalking technique, which achieves a longer stride by rotating the hips more. Imagine fitting one extra step into the time you usually take to move ten paces. Your stride will be a bit shorter, and you'll need to swing your arms a bit more vigorously (bending them at the elbows a bit more than usual will help). Because you're moving a little faster, those extra steps eventually will burn a few extra inches off of you.

Moving faster can also affect your mental state. If

you're feeling down, the extra effort will release a few more of the chemicals in the brain that help block pain. Striding along can make you feel powerful, active, energized. I've learned that when I'm down, walking off the blues reverses my mood more thoroughly than candy— and if I do go after those Raisinets later, at least I don't feel as guilty. Usually, though, the craving subsides, replaced by a whole-body sense of well-being.

Pick up your pace, and pick up your spirits.

Take Things in Stride

If you're walking for exercise, you already know that a healthy pace keeps your heart beating fast enough to do you good. You want to keep moving without letting small irregularities in the ground slow you down. But how do you do that, especially if you're walking in the city where you may be constantly stepping on and off the curb or trying to avoid obstacles?

Some hikers seem to have no problems going down steep hills; others move more gingerly. One of the differences between the two is that the hikers who are most comfortable try to keep an even pace regardless of what's happening with the terrain below their feet. It's easier to do that if you think of your legs as rocking your weight back and forth between them, each leg absorbing your weight in turn. For a smooth, flowing stride, extend your leg but don't lock your knees tightly, and let your foot roll forward from heel to toe as you shift your weight. Think of your hip as carrying your body instead of your leg; this cushions the shift from leg to leg, and small obstacles—curbs, small rocks, bumps in the road—aren't as likely to catch you off-balance. You're steadier on your feet and able to keep an easy, even rhythm in your walk. If you're going downhill, your knees will probably be more bent than usual, but try to stay as upright as possible, letting your legs do the work instead of your back.

As you walk, feel the resilience in your legs. Think of their ability to cope with the small jolts of a ragged, uneven surface as a metaphor for the ability to overcome the stings of everyday life. Too often, the feeling a friend calls being "pecked to death by ducks" keeps us off-balance, waiting for the next upset. As you move steadily over the ground, keeping your pace regardless of what's in the path, revel in your ability to take things in stride—literally.

Relax Your Neck

Chances are when you start a walk, you'll be carrying some baggage—or at least your shoulders will look as if you are. Tight with tension you're not even aware of, they have a distinct tendency to sneak upward toward your ears.

The shoulders and neck, which have the job of holding the head up straight, often are the magnet for all the stress in our bodies. We seem to want to withdraw ourselves into the chest, unconsciously pulling our shoulders forward to shield ourselves from the outside world. To break the habit, you have to work at relaxing your shoulders and neck as you walk, even if you've stretched at the beginning. When you do, you almost automatically stand up straighter and pull in your stomach.

As you walk, focus on pulling your shoulders down for a few seconds. Roll them in time with your step to loosen the muscles. Think about lengthening your spine from the top down, reaching your head straight up from the back of the neck (don't just raise the chin!). As you do, take some deep breaths. This will loosen the muscles in your chest, which tend to be too tight, and let the muscles of the upper back help get your neck in proper position.

Doing this at the beginning of your walk not only helps get your body in good alignment, but can also help you relax mentally. Just as the mind can cause the shoulders and neck to tense, so can the process work in reverse. You'll find your head clearing, freeing up mental energy to contemplate your surroundings and find inspiration as you walk.

Feel the Beat of the Feet

There is something about rhythm that is instinctively comforting. We are drawn to it from the moment we can pound out a beat. It's in our animal natures; I remember watching my dog hypnotize himself by rocking gently back and forth as his paws kneaded an old blanket.

Like a repeated chant, the one-two of our feet hitting the pavement can have the same effect that the blanket-kneading did on my dog. Just as gentle rocking can help calm an infant, the rhythm of our steps comforts our minds.

As work requires more and more mental effort, our bodies too often become what novelist Douglas Coupland calls "**meat puppets.**" The term sneers at the physical being as merely a poor cousin to the brain— the only organ alleged to have any real significance in an age of more involvement with our machines and less with the natural world.

The natural rhythm of walking works against that division of body and mind. Kinesthesia is the sense of your own motion; you know you're walking because your muscles tell your brain so. Kinesthesia demonstrates the close connection between the two, and it's one reason why walking's left/right cadence can affect our mental state. Whether you're listening to music on a portable cassette player or simply feeling the beat of your own stride, let the rhythm unify your body and spirit.

Six Steps In, Six Steps Out

Take a truly deep breath. Hold it for a second or two. Now let it all out slowly. Feel more relaxed, a bit calmer?

Breathing rhythmically and slowly has long been a way to combat tension and repair tattered nerves. In some cultures, it is tied to religious practice (think of Zen meditation techniques). Many yoga practitioners believe that deliberately changing the normal pattern of breathing also changes your state of mind, eliminating distractions and helping to focus your mental energy more clearly on a chosen subject. Some strive to breathe as little as six times per minute. Clearly six breaths a minute is not designed to be used with an exercise routine—you wouldn't get enough oxygen—but you can use the same sort of measured, rhythmic breathing at a faster rate as you walk to help reduce stress. If you walk with headphones and a tape player, you may already match your stride to the music, but you don't need a tape to get a good beat going.

As you walk, count to six as you inhale slowly, taking one step on each count; after six steps, your lungs should be fully expanded. Now exhale during your next six steps. Repeat the six-step inhale and six-step exhale as you walk, for as long as you feel comfortable doing so. You'll be breathing more deeply, clearing out stale air and increasing your lung capacity. If six counts doesn't feel right, try counting to four or eight. The important thing is to take good, deep breaths in a steady rhythm.

Because this breathing exercise can help channel your mental energies, this is an especially good way to start a MindWalk in which you want to think about a particular problem. The rhythm and the influx of oxygen help clear out old thought patterns that may have become repetitive, leaving your mind free to explore fresh ways of viewing a situation.

In, in, in, in, in, in. Out, out, out, out, out, out. You've got it.

The Back-up Plan

There are times when everything seems just too routine, too predictable. You've been doing the same things the same way for as long as you can remember. Bored? You betcha.

Take a tip from the Chinese. People who visit China are often astonished to see dozens of people out in public parks, cheerfully shuffling in reverse. The Chinese say it can help with back pain and improve digestion. I have no idea whether that's true; I simply like the concept as a metaphor for doing the opposite of what you're used to, which can be applied to both body and mind.

The feeling is a bit like yoga in demanding a certain mental discipline. You're usually not moving very quickly, so you have time to feel the movement of your body. If you don't want to do a full route backward—not an unreasonable feeling—it might be fun as a change of pace for a couple of minutes during a regular walk. If you want to try it, it's best to pick a flat surface in a safe place; I wouldn't recommend it on a bike path crowded with in-line skaters, but a high school track would work. You'll also need a healthy disregard for the stares you'll draw. You can simply glance backward from time to time to check the path ahead of—er, behind—you.

And maybe doing something that feels as silly as walking backward has lessons to teach about looking at life with a fresh eye, about trying new things. What might you do differently if you reversed your outlook? Maybe that means trying on someone else's perspective; maybe it means breaking a pattern that isn't working and going in the opposite direction.

Try turning your mind around today as you turn your body.

Stave Off Spasms

Tension. It makes your jaw clench, your stomach churn, your muscles contract. It may be such a chronic part of your life that most of the time you don't even notice it. The effects can be subtle from day to day; however, left unattended, it builds up in the body's out-of-the-way places.

The problem is compounded when you don't get the exercise that can help wring that tension out of your muscles. Then one day you bend a little too far or twist something a little too much, and wham! The muscle seizes up and refuses to budge. It's called a spasm, but it feels like an iron clamp pinching your bones, leaving you rigid and unable to move.

Walking regularly helps discharge a lot of that physical tension before it gets a chance to accumulate. An exercised muscle is flexible, better able to cope with the little wrench or strain that can send a taut muscle into spasm. Each walk leaves your body a little more toned, a little more resilient. Think of it as if you were gently opening the twist-off top of a bottle of soda. Releasing the pressure inside a little at a time prevents a major eruption and soda all over the floor; releasing muscle tension regularly keeps it from building to the point that you seize up.

When you go for your walk today, imagine all that accumulated tension hissing out of you like the pressure from an opened soda bottle. As the jingle used to say, it's the pause that refreshes.

Your Mental Walking Wardrobe

One of the things we get to do when we walk is to let our fantasies roam along with our feet. Just as the act of writing something down helps you remember it even without having to refer to what you've written, so can physical movement that is graceful or powerful create a similar mental state. You probably have a particular outfit that makes you feel like a million bucks every time you wear it. The way you walk can do the same.

It's fun to move as though you were the person you want or hope to be. If your confidence needs boosting, picture yourself as chairman of the board of your own company, your shoes clicking imperiously across marble floors into the boardroom as you prepare to take charge of the agenda.

Or imagine yourself as a prowling cougar, your muscles sleek and moving effortlessly underneath your skin. You don't have to be on all fours to experience the alert, cautious motion of a cat on the hunt. Perhaps you're a conductor coming on stage to give the downbeat to a symphony orchestra. Or a horse loping easily across the grass. Or a sultry Latin dancer who knows she attracts the eyes of the men who pass on the street. Or an Olympic diver striding up to the edge of the board, feet padding as easily along the narrow space as on a familiar wide sidewalk.

Whatever imagined walking identity you choose, let it be one that creates a sense of physical assurance. The body has an amazing memory. Rehearsing a powerful body language can prove useful when you're in a situation that calls for that strength; your body's kinesthetic memory—yes, the muscles have the ability to remember movement—can reinforce the confidence you need at that moment. As you let your walk subtly reflect that imagined personality, so will your mental state begin to take on the power of your body—even if it's only a temporarily borrowed body.

Develop a wardrobe of MindWalks, and let your body teach itself to carry your wildest dreams.

Beating the 4:30 Fade-out

You know the feeling: You just can't seem to get going. You drink some coffee to kick your brain into "alert," but you're still moving in slow motion. Call it what you will—the blahs, a slump—suddenly you realize that you have all the energy of a sea slug. It's the sedentary version of what runners call "hitting the wall," and too often we take it as a cue to head for the nearest dose of fat or sugar.

Experiment for a couple of weeks by keeping a log of the times you feel sluggish. You'll probably find that there's a certain time of day when it tends to hit. For most people, it's around 4:30 p.m., but your energy may choose late morning or just after lunch to go on strike. Once you know when your metabolism tends to slow down, you can plan to take a five- to ten-minute walk to revive yourself.

A brisk pace is invigorating, but don't get so focused on speed that you ignore the world around you. After all, a certain amount of the mental slump probably results from your brain having one-too-many fastballs pitched at it. Most of the time we handle whatever comes at us with the logical, verbal side of our brains. A few minutes spent in a more intuitive mode—noticing colors, shapes, sensations—can help get us back in the batter's box.

Deliberately take a few deep breaths before you set out. The oxygen boost can jump-start your failing concentration, allowing you to absorb your surroundings more fully. Usually it will take only a few minutes of mental and physical relief to refuel.

Take a walk, and get back in the game.

Poetry in Motion

When I was in high school, everyone in my twelfth-grade English class had to recite from heart the Prologue to Chaucer's *The Canterbury Tales* —in Middle English. It was one of those experiences that marks you for life. For most of us, the assignment was a coupling of sheer determination and the desire to graduate. We're talking 42 lines of "Whan that Aprille with his shoures soote/the droghte of March hath perced to the roote ...." How to remember stuff that bore only a teasing resemblance to the English spoken by a Tennessee teenager?

The only way was to let the Doggerel Effect work a little magic. You know the Doggerel Effect. It's the ability of a particular rhythm to camp out in our heads like an unwanted guest who won't go away. Getting into the beat was the only way I could hope to memorize Chaucer: "Whan that A-prille with his shou-res soo-te the droghte of March hath per-ced to the roo-te." (In case your Middle English is a little rusty, that's "When April with its sweet showers has pierced to the root the drought of March.") Endless repetitions stitched the words into my brain; to this day I can rattle off the first 12 lines at high speed, simply because of the "DA da DA da DA da Da da DA da."

When I found myself walking one day with the Prologue loping through my head, I realized that poetry is a perfect accompaniment to a MindWalk. A pronounced rhythm can help keep you keep up your pace. Unlike an audiotape, reciting in your head leaves you open to your surroundings, and you can turn off the recitation whenever you run out of memory. Plus you'll be able to amaze your friends with your mastery of something completely useless.

I've also gotten stuck on the first few lines of "Evangeline" (another high-school leftover: "This is the for-est prim-e-val ..."). Anything with a bounce will do: a limerick, a nursery rhyme, a rock lyric. Check out *Committed to Memory: 100 Best Poems to Memorize*, edited by John Hollander (Riverhead Books, $12) if you need inspiration.

Let poetry move you.

THINKING THINGS THROUGH

Solvitur ambulando.
(It is solved by walking.)

St. Augustine

Getting to "Aha!"

Sometimes the best way to think about a mental challenge is not to think—at least not with our conscious minds.

We all know the feeling of turning something over in our heads without getting any closer to a solution; our brain, like a well-trained pack mule, keeps plodding along the same worn grooves. To break the pattern, you need to give the pack mule a rest and put the intuitive part of your brain to work. Many creative people rely on walks to stimulate their thought processes. "I can only meditate when I am walking," said 18th-century philosopher Jean-Jacques Rousseau. "When I stop I cease to think; my mind only works with my legs."

There's a physiological reason why walking can bring on new insights; you are literally on a different wavelength from the way you usually operate. Most of the time, our brains generate beta waves to help us cope with stress, think analytically, communicate, and process the sights, sounds, and sensations of the world around us. These beta waves move fast; we have roughly four-teen to thirty of them each second. However, the rhythm of walking can induce the brain to move from a beta state into an alpha state. When you're experiencing alpha waves, which occur only about eight to thirteen times a second, your mind is more relaxed and you're more inwardly focused. Because alpha waves aren't busy processing so much external input, they open the door to creativity, to the part of the brain that often gets plowed under when it is trying to cope with problems of logic and language.

To prepare your subconscious, first give it the raw materials it needs to work with. As you're warming up for your walk, summarize the problem in your mind, as if you were handing your subconscious a folder with all the necessary information. Refresh your memory about the circumstances that have led you to where you are now. If you're facing a major decision, briefly review the options available and the advantages and disadvantages of each.

Then put your mind on autopilot. Don't force your mind to go over the same terrain it's already worn itself out on. Instead, focus on your surroundings. Feel the breeze on your face. Concentrate on the rhythm and sensations of walking itself, or on your breathing. Paying attention to your senses and your physical self can help still the voice inside your head and let the alpha waves kick in while your unconscious keeps chugging away in the background, much as it does when you're asleep. Let your pack-mule brain amble away from the same old track and onto more fertile ground, where it can find something to really munch on.

The result of such effortless, unforced thought is often an inspiration so clear that you wonder why it wasn't obvious before. It's what some people call the "Eureka!" experience. As you walk today, free your subconscious to give you a mental slap on the forehead.

Train the Monkey

You're walking along trying to focus on the beauty around you, trying to simply be still inside and meditate on your surroundings. Or maybe you're trying to tackle a problem and want to concentrate. Ah, but your mind has a mind of its own; you just can't seem to shut it up. It keeps wandering off the subject, chattering like mad about that errand you forgot to run ... the meeting coming up at work ... what to fix for dinner tonight ... the bill that needs paying with money you don't have ... dinner ... no time ... phone call ... You get the picture.

You've got a case of "monkey mind." A great image, isn't it? It's a phrase used by Zen meditation masters for those times when your attention leaps frantically from place to place, jabbering away and going anywhere but where you want it. All this activity is a natural function for the brain, but it can be highly distracting, whether you're trying to concentrate or simply want to listen to that quiet voice inside you.

To control monkey mind, you first need to notice that it's happening. As you walk along, monitor your thoughts, watching for the times when you begin to drift into frenzied thought. Think of the monkey as being on a leash; when you notice him wandering off, rein him in gently, bringing your thoughts back to where you want them. Monitoring the leaps make it easier to get your focus back quickly. As you do this, you're training your "monkey mind" to obey you.

It takes years of practice to train the monkey, but the more you observe the way your mind works, the better behaved it will be. And the less monkey chatter, the more you'll be able to hear the voice of your true spirit.

Live by the 80/20 Rule

When we feel overwhelmed, it's usually because of the pain-in-the-neck stuff: chores, errands, cleaning the house (though I tend to agree with someone who once said, "Why bother cleaning up? You only have to do it again next year!"). At work there are the presentations, the reports, the meaningless meetings, the paperwork. But occasionally we also can feel overwhelmed by the good stuff—the infinite number of choices of things we'd love to do if only we had the time and money. Should we go to this weekend's harvest festival? Save the money and splurge a year from now on a longer trip? Spend the time to visit family, or take preliminary steps toward starting a small home-based business? Decisions, decisions.

I've come up with a simple guide for helping me make those choices. It's based on a rule of thumb used in business, which states that 80 percent of the impact of something will come from 20 percent of it. For example, 80 percent of the revenue of a business may come from only 20 percent of its customers. Or 80 percent of the complaints about a product may come from 20 percent of its features. To use your resources most effectively, you focus on the 20 percent who represent your best customers, or solve the one problem that's causing 80 percent of your complaints.

The formula can work just as well for getting the greatest reward from your personal life. We're all too pressed for time to do everything, but that doesn't mean necessity should make all the choices. Instead of letting yourself be distracted by too many options, or letting exhaustion select the ever-popular default choice of flopping down in front of the TV, try prioritizing activities using the 80/20 rule.

If you were to spend 80 percent of your free time— even if that's only ten minutes a day—on the 20 percent of your activities that give you the most pleasure or that move you in the direction you want to go, what would they be? As you walk, make a mental list. Then select the ones that consistently give you the biggest payback, the ones that will provide 80 percent of your happiness if you have to do without the rest.

What's in your top 20? Spending more time with children? Browsing antique stores? Reading? Walking? Gardening? If you're dieting, which forbidden foods will give you 80 percent of the pleasure you crave if you allow yourself to eat them as a treat on special occasions? If 80 percent of what's good about life comes from cleaning the house, then put that high on the list; if not, think about just how much time it really deserves.

You'll always make new discoveries as you grow, and you can revise the list any time you want. But the 80/20 rule can help you enjoy life more because you're spending more time on the things that truly mean the most to you.

You can also use the 80/20 rule to help you resolve conflicts and solve problems. I'll bet if you thought about all the things that are troubling you, you'd probably realize that solving 20 percent of them—the biggest, the nastiest, the most worrisome—would eliminate 80 percent of the stress. Focus on that 20 percent, and let the rest go for the time being. That way, rather than being diffused, your energy will be directed toward your most important target like a laser beam.

As you walk today, pick your top-20 list and think about how you can focus your efforts on those items. And I'll let you in on a secret: 80 percent of the benefit of the whole process will come from simply making the list.

Life in Balance

Walking is such a common activity that we take it for granted. As we put one foot after another in a familiar cadence—left, right, left, right—we don't think much about what we're doing.

Alternating your weight between your two feet is simply a matter of keeping your balance. You push off from one foot to be safely caught by the other in a movement so natural we don't even think about it. We don't sense that we're really doing the same thing as high-wire artists in the circus: keeping ourselves upright and moving forward without falling to left or right. If you were to stop in mid-stride and rely only on the leg you're currently using, you would lose your balance.

As you walk along, meditate on the way in which the physical movement of walking reflects life. Think of the physical trade-off between left and right as an outward manifestation of spiritual balance, of the interplay of opposing forces. We all feel sometimes as though we're pulled in opposite directions. Life is full of yin/yang propositions: the conscious vs. the unconscious, the emotional vs. the logical, duty vs. desire. Both ends of the spectrum have their place.

As you walk, imagine the interaction between your feet as a logical balance. Left needs right to keep you moving forward, and right needs left. Though they're working in opposition, the two actually function together to get you where you're going. Use your walk as a metaphor. Focus on how conflicting sides can complement each other, just as two legs support a single direction. As you fall under the calming spell of a MindWalk, your subconscious can go to work on a problem, generating alternative ways of dealing with conflict besides letting the battle rage. Reconciling warring factions in your spirit will lead to an inner equilibrium that feels as comfortable as the physical one created by left, right, left, right.

Let both sides work in harmony.

Your Family Resource Bank

Part of discovering the extraordinary in the everyday is realizing the resources we have that we don't even think about most of the time. When I'm feeling down, I try to remember some of the people to whom I'm related and the qualities that I admire in them.

My mother, for example, would not seem to many people to be anyone extraordinary; when I was growing up, I saw her only as housewife and mother. And yet she also was one of the brave women who nursed soldiers wounded in the days after the invasion of Normandy during World War II. I've also watched her battle back from a heart attack, triple-bypass surgery, and a broken hip; she seemed to worry most about how her health problems would affect others. I have an aunt in her 80s who never ceases to inspire me with her sharp mind and her restless curiosity. I like to think that somewhere in my makeup are those same qualities—my mom's courage and selflessness, my aunt's spirit of adventure—ready to be called on when I need them.

As you walk, think about your genetic resource bank. What family traits would you like to think you've inherited? Your dad's organizational ability? Your grandmother's rapport with nature? You may already be aware of some shared characteristics, but contemplating a relative's life may help you discover other personality traits you'd like to be able to rely on in yourself. Nature lets very little go to waste; think of a beloved family member's personality living on through you.

And let's face it: Your family probably also has plenty of qualities that you want no part of. But who needs reminding of flaws that have been part of your life since childhood? Sometimes adjusting the way you think about them helps (see "Flip Your Attitude"). You might realize that the nagging that made you miserable as a kid was part of a parent's overall persistence or determination to make things perfect. As painful as it may have been to endure when you were growing up, that same kind of determination could prove useful if you can adopt it yourself selectively in pursuit of your own goals.

Rummage through your extended family's storehouse of character traits; you'll probably find some you want to dust off and claim as your own.

The 3-D Question

You've had an "Aha!" moment: Your walk has helped your brain turn up an answer to a problem. But your walk isn't finished—and maybe your idea isn't, either. You've got to keep on walking to get home; why not try doing the same with your idea? Whatever solution you've come up with may be perfectly good, but it's probably not the only one that will work. Pushing past your first response can generate more choices, which often are more creative than your first acceptable one.

An easy way to do this is to ask yourself what I call a "3-D question." The same question asked in three different ways can give your brain a new perspective. For example, let's say you're trying to figure out how you can balance work and family demands. You ask yourself, "How can I spend more time with the kids without hurting my performance at work?" The second question might be, "How can I maintain the same income while spending more time at home?" And a third: "How can I keep my boss happy and still care for my kids?" All three get at the same issue: wanting to be a better parent while continuing to earn a living.

But the way each one is phrased could lead to different answers. Question 1 might suggest getting up early to be with the kids before you go to work. Question 2 might lead you to think of looking for another job, or finding a way to earn money in your spare time by doing something that the kids could help you with. And Question 3 might suggest a discussion with your boss about a more flexible work schedule.

Just as you may not discover one thing that makes your walk special until the end, sometimes the answers you have to dig for are more fruitful than the ones that sprout first. Keep walking, think in 3-D, and discover just how far you can really go.

Think Feet, Not Eat

The urge always seems to be there. You get up out of your chair and auto-shuffle toward the refrigerator. You know you're not hungry, but the sooner you polish off those leftovers from last night, the sooner you'll be able to start that diet, right? Sure you will.

Restlessness, sadness, and anxiety all often masquerade as hunger. Buried emotions take on new life in our stomachs, leading us into the kitchen to wander from cabinet to cabinet in search of the unknown thing that will satisfy our cravings. If we're at work, a particular treat from the vending machine can start to look like the Holy Grail. The problem is, the cravings aren't really for food, so no matter what we eat, it's never the right thing.

When you find yourself exploring the kitchen like a treasure hunter without a map, maybe it's time to use your feet to help you feed the hunger that's based in your head, not your stomach. Drink a glass of water and head outdoors. Focus on your surroundings, using some of your favorite MindWalk techniques. That simple shift of attention can distract you enough to give the hunger pangs a chance to subside—if indeed they were truly there to begin with. Let's face it: Most of us know when we're eating because we're really hungry and when we're eating because of something that's bothering us. We just don't listen to ourselves closely enough. Walking amplifies the scathingly honest inner voice that, try as we might, we can't really fool.

As you walk, feel your muscles getting leaner and your body getting slimmer because of the combination of exercise and self-restraint. I'm not suggesting you try this at midnight; those wee-hours binges need another solution. But when you know that what you crave won't be found in the kitchen cabinet, the vending machine, or the food court, try to think "feet" instead of "eat."

Out of Your Head

The scientists call it "ruminating." It's the process of going over and over the same thoughts with no productive outcome. Maybe you're worried about some imagined threat. Maybe you're obsessing about a wrong someone's done you. Maybe your inner disciplinarian is beating up on you for all your myriad faults, real or imagined. You're like a dog with a favorite ratty old chew toy; your brain gets a good grip on the object of your obsession and gnaws away at it.

Often you're not even aware that you're ruminating until you suddenly realize, as if being jerked awake, that you've been covering the same ground for the last half-hour with no progress. When that happens, it's time for a MindWalk. Getting outdoors and moving is like pulling the chew toy away from the dog. It breaks the cycle of obsessive thought and gives the poor, tired brain new rabbits to chase. Your eyes, your ears, your muscles begin to send messages from your environment that force you into a more outward focus.

Walking, you may still find yourself thinking about whatever is causing your brain to chase its own tail. But just as walking moves you forward physically, so is it likely to at least produce some results from all that mental activity. In spite of itself, the mind begins to come up with solutions, fresh approaches, a more realistic perspective. Circular thought patterns begin to spiral outward in new directions.

Go for a walk, and get out of your head.

MANAGING STRESS

To all who feel overwhelmed and work-weary,
the exhilarating exercise of walking offers
both a stimulus and a sedative.

ROBERT LOUIS STEVENSON

Match Your Steps to Your Stress

We experience two different types of stress—one mental, one physical—and different types of MindWalks work in different ways to help us cope with each one.

Mental tension is caused by negative thought patterns. We torture ourselves with feelings of inadequacy, worry about imagined disasters ahead, or get depressed. These highly charged emotions block the release of endorphins, the brain chemicals designed to soothe and calm us; your mind is like a racing, oil-starved engine that has no place to go and eventually burns out. When we're under this kind of mental tension, we tend to snap at our spouse or kids and slam the door shut as we walk out.

Then there's physical stress: the so-called "fight or flight" response, developed through the centuries as humans survived by either defeating harm or running away from it. When we feel threatened, our body is flooded with adrenaline, which gives us the energy to combat the threat or flee. However, evolution intended adrenaline to be a quick-response mechanism. When it becomes a permanent reaction to daily stress, we end up perpetually drained.

The two types aren't mutually exclusive, of course; one is often brought on by the other. But try attacking each type with a walking pace that addresses its unique characteristics.

If your tension is largely mental, try walking at a calm, relaxed pace. What you want is to move your brain toward a peaceful alpha state, to open the floodgates to those endorphins. Deliberately walk more slowly than you might otherwise. Clear your mind by paying attention to your immediate surroundings instead of dwelling on whatever is causing your tension. Focusing on externals instead of on your internal stressors will allow your brain to recover, to step away from the problem long enough to calm down. Deep breathing is also helpful. This slower pace relaxes the body, which in turn sends an automatic signal to the brain: "Hey, chill out! We're takin' a break here!"

When you're feeling physical stress—your muscles are tight, your palms are sweaty, your mouth is dry—walking briskly can help burn off the adrenaline-induced energy causing your symptoms. When you're really ticked off, when you wake up anxious from the vague terrors of half-sleep, when you dread a major confrontation—that's the time to get out and really move.

Both types of walks help you fight stress, but depending on your frame of mind, you may find one more effective than the other. You also can combine them in the same walk. Start out fast to burn off emotional overload, then slow down and feel a sense of calm settle into your bones.

Aaaahh.

Get Out of Dodge

You just can't seem to concentrate. Your muscles are tense. You're tired. In short, you're stressed. Evolution has provided our bodies with a handy thermometer for taking our psychic temperature. When our palms get sweaty, our face flushes, our heart rate speeds up, we know our bodies are screaming, "Lemme at him!" or "Lemme outta here!"

Sometimes it seems as though life requires one long dose of adrenaline just to keep going. And God's sense of irony is such that the moments of greatest stress are precisely the times when poor judgment can cause the most damage.

When you feel the symptoms of stress—like daily? —it's time to take a tip from the old movie gunslingers and get out of Dodge. The "flight" part of the "fight or flight" equation doesn't have to mean abandoning the field entirely. A ten-minute walk can give you the psychological stamina to get back in the fight with greater reserves of energy.

An experiment with lab rats, performed by Dr. Hans Selye, demonstrated that exercise can fortify both mind and body. Selye subjected ten rats to blinding lights, electric shocks, and constant noise—in other words, stress. (Why does this remind me of living in New York City?) Within a month, all ten were dead. Another ten rats were put through the same hell—but only after they had gone on a rigorous aerobics program on a little rat treadmill. A month later, they were all alive and healthy —though I suspect more than a little ticked off.

When you feel as though your life is a rerun of *Gunfight at the OK Corral*, get out of Dodge for a few minutes and walk around. It can help prevent you from shooting yourself in the foot.

Learn Strength from Sorrow

Sometimes it seems as if all the sadness of the world has landed on your shoulders. It may be a sudden loss or a gradual silting-up of depression that blocks our connections to the world. Much as we feel like curling up in a fetal position, walking is a much better antidote for the blues. Motion swabs the brain with the biochemicals that act as its own natural antidepressants, which help numb the pain in a healthier way than any chemical substitute.

Walking won't cure your problems (though it can improve your problem-solving abilities). And it's no substitute for professional help if you need it. However, it can help subdue some of the chaos that swirls inside you. Unlike a workout at the gym, walking doesn't put a lot of physical demands on your body at a time when you may not feel like moving at all. If you want to shuffle along numbly, that's OK; nobody will think anything of it.

If you're just getting started, think of a walking program as something good you can create for yourself. It can't eliminate a sense of loss, but it can remind you that good things can still come into your life to help counterbalance the losses we all inevitably suffer. If you can learn to pay attention to your surroundings as you walk, the kind of small MindWalk discoveries we've talked about can provide a welcome if momentary distraction from the ache inside.

As you walk, your response to the world will naturally be colored by your emotions. You may find yourself comparing what you see and hear to situations or people in your life, drawing metaphors based on what's going on inside you. You may see the generosity of a loved one in the abundance of a flowerbed, or find an example of the strength you desperately need in a tree root that has managed to split a sidewalk. Gradually, your heart will begin to use natural materials all around you as textbooks that teach you how to cope with your sorrow.

Walking is the perfect time to meditate on what you can take away from this dark time. Part of what makes pain so painful is that it often appears senseless. Trying to decipher the lessons life may be forcing us to learn at least offers hope that there is something to be gained from our suffering.

Try to find a spot that's relatively private, where the tears can roll down your cheeks if they need to. This is your time to mourn. Sometimes life requires simply putting one foot in front of the other. Sometimes it's enough just to keep moving.

Look Fear in the Face

Some days you wake up and dread the thought of getting out of bed. That instinctive desire to crawl back into the womb is often a response to fear. In your half-awake state, you may be conscious of nothing more than a vague unease, something as simple as "Not another day of ___" (fill in the blank for yourself). But if you lie still a minute, clear your mind, and listen to what's really going on inside you, you may find that it's not sloth but anxiety that's been silently gnawing at you as you slept. Psychologists have found that feelings of helplessness and frustration often stem from buried fear of one's inability to cope with imaginary disaster.

This is precisely the time to get up and go for a MindWalk. Left unchallenged, fear is like a fertilized egg deep inside a woman's body. It divides and divides again, reproducing itself endlessly until it grows from a tiny cell into Rosemary's Baby, a monster child within that leaves you exhausted and immobile.

Get moving. The exercise revs up your adrenaline and endorphins. If you're feeling exhausted, all the more reason you need to recruit these powerful allies to help you fight what's bothering you. Don't walk away from your feelings, though; otherwise, you'll be in the same situation the next morning—and the next and the next. Walk with your feelings, but reassert control of them as you go.

Focus on your anxiety long enough to identify what's really causing it. Usually there is some ultimate outcome you're worried about. If it's problems on the job—let's say you're worried about whether a report was OK—the ultimate outcome you fear may be job loss. At home, worry about the reaction of a loved one may stem from a half-acknowledged fear of losing his or her love. The more you can define what's really causing your state of mind, the easier it is to address it.

Force yourself to imagine the worst thing that can happen. Will you lose your home? Your job? Get a divorce? Be unable to pay your bills? As you walk, imagine the dread you feel as a concrete physical sensation—the proverbial butterflies in your stomach, perhaps. Feel the tremors of their wings beating against your muscles. Or imagine a backpack loaded with rocks. Feel the burden on your shoulders as you walk; experience the dead weight, the way it slows you down. Mentally locate your fear in a specific place on or in your body.

Then get rid of it. Take several deep breaths and exhale some of those butterflies each time until they're gone and you can feel your stomach muscles relaxing. Lift and relax your shoulders, shrug off the backpack, and let it slip to the ground behind you. Walk on, free of the strain of your anxiety. Feel how much easier you move with the new lightness in your step.

You've already imagined the worst that can happen. Now, free of your fear, you're ready to force yourself to come up with a worst-case solution. If you lose your job, would you get another one? Change careers? Start your own business? Live in a smaller place to cut expenses? You might not have all the answers by the end of your walk, but chances are you'll have thought of at least one thing you could do to make your situation better—if indeed the worst case ever comes true. As potential plans of action come to you, your fear will recede even further. Knowing you have a game plan for the worst makes it easier to face the not-quite-so-bad. Be sure your solutions phase is at least half of your scheduled walk.

As you head back, remind yourself that you had the courage to get out of bed and walk toward your problems instead of away from them. Having done this reinforces your image of yourself as a fighter, a problem-solver rather than a victim. You had the spirit and energy to get moving; you can use that same spirit and energy to attack what's bothering you.

And as you walk, remember this quote from Eleanor Roosevelt: "You gain strength, courage, and confidence by every experience in which you really stop to look fear in the face."

Get Back to Reality

When you need money desperately, nothing is more exciting than the possibility of actually getting some. I remember getting a phone call one morning about a project that would not only bring me some money but that might possibly give me my long-awaited fifteen minutes of fame. If I got back to the caller quickly, I would have an answer in an hour or so about whether the project was a go. I zipped off an e-mail answer; then came the wait while my ideas were presented at a meeting.

I was so excited that all the blood seemed to leave my hands and clot in the pit of my stomach. I mean, I was breathing-hard, wet-the-pants, want-to-scream, jump-up-and-down excited. I could see the yacht pulling up to the dock before my very eyes. But I wasn't going to find out anything for at least a couple of hours—and in the meantime I was no more capable of getting any work done than I was of captaining the Starship Enterprise.

What to do? Go for a walk, naturally. I burst out of the house at a fast trot, my mind buzzing with hope and anxiety. What if this led to all sorts of other work? What was happening at that meeting? What if? What if? Too much of a (potentially) good thing was driving me nuts.

As I walked, the roar in my head began to recede. I reminded myself that it wasn't the end of the world if the deal didn't happen; I'd be no worse off than I had been at the start of the day. The rhythm of my breathing eased the tension in my chest. My mind turned to the project I'd been working on when the call came, and I got a couple of good ideas for it. By the time I finished my walk, I was able to sit back down at my desk with a clear head, steady hands, and the possibilities—both good and bad—in better perspective.

If I hadn't taken my dreams out for a little stroll with reality, I might have sunk into despair when my contact finally called back and the answer was disappointing. But because my walk had helped discharge a lot of that frantic, nervous energy, I was able to go right back to work.

Managing your moods doesn't always have to mean cheering up. Sometimes walking is just as effective when it's calming you down.

Let It Go

Want to get a good workout, to really steam along? Try going for a walk when you're already steaming. The energy you generate while you're marching along seething over that thoughtless comment from a spouse, that scheming colleague, that clueless boss, can turn off the burner beneath your boiling temper— or at least help reduce the boil to a slow simmer.

One of the hallmarks of emotional maturity, according to psychologist Daniel P. Goleman in his book, *Emotional Intelligence*, is the ability to calm oneself, to keep the pressure cooker of emotional distress from exploding all over the place. Walking lets you get out there and do something physical about whatever is bothering you without suffering the consequences of actually punching someone in the snoot (which, of course, is what you really want to do).

Better to take all that rage and translate it into the energy needed to fuel a good pace. I find that punching the air from time to time with my arms as I walk gives not only an extra aerobic boost but the gratifying sense of delivering a series of good hard air wallops to whatever (or whoever) is causing the smoke to come out of my ears. (You might want to save your Evander Holyfield routine for areas where you won't find yourself explaining to the police, "But I was just doing an anger walk!")

A more subdued but still effective way to release emotion is to visualize it as a physical object. Imagine taking all the anger you've released by walking and compacting it into a chunk lodged deep inside you (you know that spot where you feel tied up in knots?). Mentally drain all the feelings that are coursing throughout your body and squeeze them into a heavy, hard little ball, the way you might pack down a snowball (another chance to do some mental smacking around).

Once you've gotten your rage well collected, imagine taking that tightly packed ball from the pit of your stomach and mentally flinging it away as hard as you can. Pick a target on the horizon and use your psychic muscles to really hurl the ball in that direction. You want to feel it leaving your hand, to watch it arc over the trees or buildings and slowly drop out of sight. You're literally putting some distance between yourself and the emotion that's overwhelming you, giving you some space to regain stability. You're not denying your anger; you're simply not letting it take charge.

Feel the sense of release, of cleansing that comes

from ridding yourself—at least temporarily—of your fury. Sometimes one throw is enough; sometimes you're mentally pitching an entire World Series. If you're a golfer, you might prefer to imagine hitting a tee shot that sails into the next county (with no slice). Just get the anger you've summoned up as far away as you can.

Walking off anger can help release the tension that your body unconsciously generates to deal with strong emotion. You're calmer, more in control, more able to deal with the problem—maybe even more able to solve it.

Have the Last Word

W hy do we always think of the perfect thing to say immediately after the opportunity has passed to say it? We stew and fret, fingering in our head for hours the snippets of an old argument. For many of us, having the last word is like having the last piece of leftover pie —it only happens late at night when we're alone.

Walking provides a perfect opportunity to finish up old arguments, to tell someone off without suffering the consequences. If you want to get the last word—finally, unquestionably, triumphantly—try doing it mentally as you walk along. I'm not recommending you walk along chattering to yourself unless you enjoy stares from strangers. And you don't want to use mental conflicts simply to duck real ones, or give up when you're justified in fighting back. But letting yourself win an argument in your head is better than simply replaying the same conversation, feeling sorry for yourself or fuming about how the other person was wrong, wrong, *wrong*.

Let 'em have it—in your head. Crush their every objection, and imagine them groveling in apology. Then let the argument come to an end while you finish your walk. You'll find that your pace has probably picked up as a result of the spillover energy. You can always choose to go back to your opponent in person if the fight is really worth pursuing. If that's your decision, your imaginary victory may have helped you exhaust some of the old emotional reactions developed in the heat of the argument. You may be ready to use a new approach or tactic. You might even decide to drop the whole thing because it's just not worth the energy.

Sometimes a silent "so there" can be just the outlet you need.

The First National Bank of You

I used to work at a financial services company. One of the first things I learned there was that small amounts of money—$5 to $10—deposited over time and left alone could end up becoming very large amounts of money.

When I began doing MindWalks regularly, I realized that they were very much like those small deposits. One by itself was a treat, but over time they began to add up to much more. I liked to walk first thing in the morning and explore my home city, discovering things I had never seen in the years I had been driving its streets. Walking in the morning gave me a different outlook on the upcoming sixteen hours. I got to plan the day in peace, turn over in my mind things I'd never get time to think about later, and align my perspective with the long-term priorities that are so easy to forget when we're hounded by daily life.

That daily MindWalk began to build my emotional reserves. When the world started to go to hell in a handbasket or a decision had to be made, I was more resilient, more conscious of what my truest self felt was most important. I began to think of each walk—each step of each walk—as a deposit of strength in my emotional bank account. When I needed to tap the account, I had the resources to draw on.

Tension is like this account's evil twin. It doesn't usually develop in an instant but gathers over time. The irritating little laugh of your coworker in the next cubicle, the skirmishes with your teenager over homework or housework, the jerk who cut you off at the start of a 30-minute commute—all bring the pressure to the explosion point. Your MindWalk can act as a pressure valve, helping you discharge small tensions before they collect and show up in the body as muscle spasms, or erupt in inappropriate ways (like blowing your stack in front of the boss).

As you walk today, imagine building your own balance of strength in your psychic account. Tension or emotional muscle: Which would you rather be adding to at the First National Bank of You?

See Beyond Today

There's a great Calvin and Hobbes cartoon, in which the kid and his imaginary tiger are sitting outdoors under a night sky. Calvin says, "Look at all the stars! The universe just goes on forever and ever!" Hobbes replies, "Kind of makes you wonder why man considers himself such a big screaming deal."

When your troubles seem overwhelming, look up. Doing so occasionally can help improve your walking form by reminding you to keep your head high. And even in a city, where buildings corral the sky into a cramped square overhead, the sky can remind us of our place in the universe. Clouds may drift along; there may be a clear swath of blue; gray thunderheads may growl threats. No matter what its temperament, the sky represents something bigger than ourselves.

Ancient people believed the gods lived among the clouds; even now, clouds are a visual shorthand for the concept of heaven. The timeless quality that inspired that belief about the sky can also help put our individual situations in perspective.

Imagine the blue stretching into infinity, with black night beyond the ozone. Galaxies are up there, worlds we can't even imagine. Or feel yourself moving under that big canopy; visualize looking down at yourself as though you were in a plane flying overhead. Do your troubles still seem as earth-shattering as they did?

If you stop to rest for a moment, play the old children's game of finding shapes in the clouds. Use them as an overhead ink-blot test that lets you create images to match your mood. As the clouds shift and reform, let your imagination sculpt from them two lovers waltzing or a valiant warrior triumphant. Mentally place a problem on a particular cloud and let the wind slowly dissolve and scatter it. Watch the clouds shift and drift, endlessly moving, reminding you that all things in the universe change.

Look up, and gaze beyond today.

A Slower Pace

So often when we walk, we walk for a reason: to lose weight, to get somewhere. We have a Purpose. That's entirely understandable given our hectic, harried lives. There are so many things on the ever-expanding To Do list that for many people, doing something just for the sake of doing it is practically considered a character flaw.

Which is precisely why we should amble occasionally when we get the chance. Ambling is entirely different from walking with a purpose: It's a MindWalk in slow motion. Ambling is slowing down to notice your surroundings, the ultimate walk-as-its-own-goal. Deliberately slowing your pace encourages contemplation of both inner and outer environments.

Ambling can be done anywhere. Nature lends itself to ambling, but so do the most unlikely places. For example, I like to amble through an office supply store. Surrounded by folders and notebooks, racks of colored pencils, and reams of paper, I have the delightful if temporary illusion that my life will dramatically improve with the purchase of the right combination of organizing tools. I crave the order they promise, the simplicity and structure that will tidy up all my many loose ends. I stand before rainbows of notepads, dazzled by the combinations of hot pink, teal, violet, and sunny yellow, like a Caribbean festival on paper.

Tropical climates invented the amble. In Key West, a walk becomes a slow-footed crawl through air as thick and warm as honey. You meander, you saunter, you stroll; anything more requires a level of effort that the sun has baked out of you. Such a deliberate pace induces a dreamy, contemplative state; the mind defers to the senses as you drift along aimlessly. The beach, with the sound of the waves as a meditative backdrop, is the perfect amble. And window-shopping is recreational urban anthropology.

The next time you get a chance, slow down and recharge.

Just Walk Away, Renee

Lots of people like to listen to tapes while they walk. Nothing wrong with that, but if you're trying to relieve stress, making your own music may be a better way to do it. Studies have shown that sounds you make —as opposed to sounds you take in—can have a profound physical effect. According to sound therapist Don Campbell, author of *The Mozart Effect*, the vibration caused by humming or chanting affects the skull and the upper-body muscles much as a massage does. Campbell recommends long, droning sounds for lowering blood pressure and stimulating circulation, but I prefer to combine humming with a good beat when I'm on a MindWalk.

I realize I'm dating myself here, but Motown was my prom music when I was a teenager, and it's not unusual for me to bounce along to "The Way You Do the Things You Do" or "My Girl." Singing may not have the same massage effect as humming, but a good tune can really get your juices going. If you don't want to do either, hit the mental cassette player. You know how you can get an annoying TV jingle stuck in your head? It's the same mechanism, but you get to choose a song you actually like.

You'll have your own picks, but here are some of mine:

Wagner's *Ride of the Valkyries*

Tommy Dorsey doing *Opus One*

Got My Own Thing Now
by the Squirrel Nut Zippers

Bonnie Raitt's *Something to Talk About*

Anything by John Phillip Sousa

The third movement of Beethoven's Ninth

Hank Williams' *Jambalaya*
("Jambalaya, crawfish pie, file gumbo...")

And—of course—the Four Seasons' *Walk Like a Man* (although I agree with whoever said that what Frankie Valli needed was to *sing* like a man). You can suit the tempo to your pace, you're in touch with what's going on around you, and you can combine the songs you want on your mental cassette.

Walk to your own different drummer.

Unlocking
your creativity

That which is creative must create itself.

John Keats

Take Your Best Shot

In your walks, have you ever come across an exquisite visual image—a particular shade of iridescent blue on a butterfly's wings, a stand of daffodils freshly opened—and said, "I wish I had a camera"? Finding such small, ephemeral treasures is one of the joys of walking. But your discoveries don't have to be lost once you've passed them by. I like to capture things I see on my walks by using my invisible camera.

It's a technique I adopted when I kept misplacing my keys. I learned that simply looking closely at the keys as I put them down—deliberately taking a mental snapshot—helped me remember where I had put them. When I began taking regular walks, I realized that my mental camera also helped me spot the small beauties that made each walk worthwhile. The photo may exist only in my mind, but it really does help make me aware of the unusual in things so ordinary we walk by them without notice. Too often we see only what we look for; an invisible camera helps us do the looking.

As you MindWalk today, think of yourself as a photographer out on a photo shoot. Your editor has turned you loose to find beautiful images (in fact, that's how photographers get some of the shots you see in magazines and newspapers; they simply wander around actively looking for them).

As you look around on your walk, think about photos you've seen: how they're composed inside a square frame, the way colors are juxtaposed to enhance each other, the attention to detail. When you see something interesting, take a moment to compose a photograph of it. Use your invisible camera to frame it. Put the subject off-center. Look at interesting patterns in leaves or buildings as striking abstract compositions. You can even put the thumbs and index fingers of both hands at right angles to form a square that can help you frame your picture before you snap your mental "shutter." Then paste the image you've captured into your heart.

You'll be surprised at how quickly your imaginary photo album will grow—and at how many more wonderful details you'll spot that you might otherwise have overlooked.

Bring Home Beauty

On my desk, I have a shallow soapstone dish filled with small treasures picked up on walks. There is a flat black rock, its smooth surface marbled with green; a horse chestnut picked up on the grounds of Van Gogh's asylum in Saint Remy; a perfect shell spiraled like a nautilus; a piece of white quartz gathered from a road bed. Perhaps my favorite is a slender animal bone found on a beach on Martha's Vineyard. Scrubbed clean by waves and sand, bleached to ivory in the sun, its smooth, curved surfaces are a delight to touch.

Walking allows you to be a scavenger of things that are too small to be noticed in the everyday rush but that have a beauty all the more special for being easily overlooked. There's still a bit of the hunter-gatherer in us; bringing things back to the cave seems to be part of our genetic makeup (anyone who doubts this has clearly never seen the crowd at a yard sale). I always try to wear something with pockets when I walk, so I can carry home new additions to the collection.

Good walking form requires that you keep your head up. However, when you're walking for inspiration as much as for exercise, being hyperaware of your surroundings can coax forth exquisite detail. Senses tuned into the natural world find wonders everywhere.

Sometimes the world's gifts are practical. On my back porch sit two benches someone else left by the street ten years ago for the garbage truck. But some of the most enjoyable discoveries will be beautiful objects you can use to decorate your home. Given time and a keen eye, you'll find yourself assembling a collection of natural artifacts that can soften a stark room or distract your eye from less-than-attractive surroundings.

Try grouping several shells in a translucent aquamarine bowl reminiscent of the sea, or lining up shells of similar shape along a windowsill. One shell is just a shell; a collection of them, grouped as they please your eye, have real presence. I've made a centerpiece of shells arranged in a circle around the edge of a simple white plate. I've created a small bouquet of blue jay feathers stuck in a small antique cream pitcher. Smooth quartz pebbles of uniform whiteness or rocks with dramatic markings can be striking. Small wildflowers often grow in the most unexpected urban areas, free for the picking; discovering a patch that has just come into bloom can be the highlight of a summer walk.

On your MindWalk, forage for objects that fit—or expand—your definition of beauty.

Color Your World

My friends laugh when I talk about how beautiful the view is from my back porch. That's because facing the yard is the rear of a five-story hospital—not exactly the ocean view I dream of having someday.

But on late summer afternoons when the sun is low in the sky, the slanting light coats the hospital walls like honey. It turns the bricks a warm red, like the rusty, iron-infused soil of the South where I grew up. The glowing bricks somehow deepen the blue of the sky behind them; the combination has the intensity of a vision. When I look out at this time of day, I'm not seeing a hospital or sky; I simply get lost in pure, rich color. What's there isn't very scenic, but what I *see* strikes my soul like a bell being rung.

Learning to truly see color instead of paying attention to what that color is on can transform a daily walk into an artist's journey. Suddenly berries are like jewels set in bushes; a rusted metal auto part by the roadside looks like a piece of soft suede. Store windows become kaleidoscopes that shift with the turn of the seasons.

On your walk today, try focusing only on colors rather than objects. Don't think of finding a beautiful flower bed; search instead for a brilliant swath of paint on the side of a house. Don't look for a view; look for a patch of rain-soaked leaves on the ground, gleaming like brown satin. If it's spring, pay attention to the shy, translucent green of the new leaves; at no other time of the year do they have that air of innocence. The quality of the light is different at different times of the year—winter tends to have a bluish cast, summer a golden one—but its effects are easy to overlook unless you're paying attention.

The time of day, the season, the weather—all can give a new drama to familiar objects. You'll see things in a new light—literally.

Temporary Treasures

We all start out as artists. Remember coloring as a kid—all the bright color combinations that the Crayola box offered? Then at some point too many of us became convinced that our drawings didn't look the way they were supposed to, and we stopped thinking visually.

Well, art is all around us. If you can find it, look at a book called *Andy Goldsworthy: A Collaboration with Nature*, a collection of photos of natural materials arranged in artful ways. Goldsworthy's elegant constructions of twigs, ice, leaves, and stones, created in outdoor settings and photographed before they disintegrate, are Zen-like in demonstrating the beauty of simple objects organized by an artist's eye.

I don't consider myself an artist, but I love to arrange things in interesting ways—interesting, at least, to me. For example, while walking on the beach at Cape Cod, some friends and I turned a forked piece of driftwood, some dried seaweed, and a couple of curved shells into an eight-inch sculpture. The driftwood formed a running body, the seaweed streamed from the top of the stick like hair, and the shell slouched at a jaunty angle on top as a cap. An exhibit free to anyone who walked by, Running Stick Man was destined to be destroyed by the next high tide.

Let your surroundings on your MindWalk inspire you to create small, temporary works of art along your path. Don't feel that they have to look like something. Try a beautiful combination of red and yellow leaves, stones with similar or contrasting colors and shapes grouped in a pattern, silky matte leaves contrasted with shiny ones— whatever pleases your eye. There is no one to judge your creations. Think of them as small ways to leave a trace of your passing without disturbing the environment.

Let your artistic soul create some secret, transitory beauty as a gift to yourself and the world.

Make Unexpected Connections

Looking for a fresh approach to a problem? On your MindWalk today, try adapting an exercise that's often used by corporations to help employees be more creative about problem-solving.

As you start your walk, select an object small enough to pick up and carry with you. It could be a leaf, a shell, a scrap of paper, a wildflower, a bottle cap. Examine it closely; this is the spark plug that's going to help you fire up your imagination. Then begin to make connections between the object and whatever problem you're stuck on. Inventing ways to relate two things that have absolutely no logical association can help you see new aspects of a situation.

Let's say you've been asked to work on a thankless project no one else seems to want to do. You spot a rock by the side of the road and decide that's your object. Then ask yourself the following questions:

How is my project like this rock?
How is my project different from the rock?
*What changes could improve both the rock
    and my project?*

At first you may have trouble coming up with

answers. That's OK; the point is to crowbar your brain out of its accustomed patterns. Eventually, you might come up with responses like these:

How is my project like this rock? They're both boring; they're not likely to go anywhere; they're not glamorous; both of them can serve as a foundation for other things.

How is my project different from the rock? The project won't last as long as the rock; the rock doesn't change, but I can be flexible about how I do my project.

What changes could improve both the rock and my project? The rock would be more useful broken into gravel; the project can be broken into smaller pieces that can be easily done by a group instead of one person.

The object you pick isn't important, and in many cases, neither are the answers. The point is to think differently about something. By forcing your brain to come up with unconventional, even silly solutions, you train it in how to be more creative in other situations. You don't have to be outdoors to do the exercise; it works just as well on a treadmill.

Unexpected connections can get your mind going as fast as your legs.

See with the Eyes of a Child

I know that getting in touch with your "inner child" is supposed to be a great thing, but I often think I'd like my inner child to shut up. I get tired of her whining when we have to get out of bed early on a cold morning, her pouting when things don't go our way, her fear of diving off life's high board. But I'm also grateful for the times when she opens my eyes to things I might not otherwise have noticed.

Small children look at things with an intensity most of us lose all too soon. They seem to examine all dimensions of an object, trying to figure out where to put it in the mental toybox that holds all the other images of things they're seeing for the first time. A child's gaze is the gaze of an artist; it sees aspects hidden from eyes that have been dulled by time and circumstance.

When you're walking, try to look at things afresh. Imagine yourself back to your own childhood, when the world could be found in a brightly colored marble. Examine small objects as a three-year-old might, picking them up and absorbing the details of texture, color, and shape. Carry your pleasures of the moment with you as you walk, tuck them into your pocket, or discard them whenever you like; a child's attention, intense while it lasts, is fleeting.

The cry of "Look, Mommy! Look what I found!" is a call to see things anew, an opportunity to refresh your eyes. If you have a child, those opportunities are built into parenthood, but even people without children can use their own memories and senses to explore the world with a child's ability to see the extraordinary in the mundane.

It beats suffering while your inner child pitches a tantrum.

Save Scraps of Inspiration

It's all too easy to lose those fleeting "Aha" moments we often experience when walking (see "A Mental Slap on the Forehead"). Other thoughts sometimes crowd in so thick and fast that we forget that momentary insight we meant to bring back with us.

Like dreams, our flashes of brilliance can be captured with a little preparation. On today's MindWalk, carry a pen and an index card with you; I like a spiral-bound notebook of index cards that can be torn out one by one. When the light bulb goes on over your head, take a moment to jot down a phrase––even a couple of words will do—to serve as a reminder when you get home. The writing only takes a few moments out of your walk, and your mind will be free to explore some more without worrying about retaining your inspiration. A pocket tape recorder, which will let you keep moving as you record your thoughts, is even better.

If you're artistically inclined and don't mind a longer interruption, you can also use index cards to do quick sketches of the miniature still lifes that appear spontaneously once you've trained your eye to look for them: a pattern of vines against a stone wall, perhaps, or a child waiting at a bus stop. Or simply note whatever made that day's walk worthwhile: the grandchild's comment that unexpectedly bubbled to memory's surface, the scrap of overheard conversation, the joke you want to remember to tell a friend.

Kept together and reviewed periodically, these reminders become a paper quilt stitched together from scraps of observation that might otherwise be lost. Start your own patchwork today.

✦

Create Your Own Songlines

Bruce Chatwin's book *Songlines* speaks about "the labyrinth of invisible pathways which meander all over Australia and are known … as 'Dreaming-tracks' or 'Songlines'."

As the ancestors of the Aborigines walked the earth long ago, so the legend goes, they created the world and everything in it—including themselves—by singing out each object's name. As they walked through what is called the Dreamtime, they left trails of song, trails that were handed down through the generations and were used as guideposts for travelers, helping them find their direction.

There has recently been some question about whether songlines actually functioned in the way Chatwin described. But whether they really are Aboriginal compasses or merely a lovely myth, songlines can serve as a metaphor for the way in which our everyday walks can help us recreate our own worlds from our dreams.

Choose a particular route and associate it with positive thoughts that help produce whatever mental result you want. For example, retrace a route you took one day when you were happy—maybe you walked with a favorite grandchild or a new love. Let the route serve as a songline for happiness: remember the good times, and dream about future joys. If you're feeling blue, take a route you walked at a time when you overcame an obstacle. Imagine reabsorbing the courage and energy you deposited for yourself along that songline.

Creating your own personal songlines can help you chart the way across your own private continent.

STAYING MOTIVATED

Above all, do not lose your desire to walk.
Every day I walk myself into a state of well-being and
walk away from every illness. I have walked myself
into my best thoughts, and I know of no thought so
burdensome that one cannot walk away from it ... if
one just keeps on walking, everything will be all right.

SOREN KIERKEGAARD

Put One Foot After Another

Runners hit The Wall. Writers get writer's block. Mothers—well, mothers often simply want to find the nearest horizontal surface and collapse on it.

There are times when it seems you just can't go on. Your life is lousy, and the future doesn't look like an improvement. On top of that, it's raining. Whether real, imagined, or inflated beyond due proportion, the challenges seem daunting. Maybe you're facing a new task for which you don't feel prepared, or perhaps a project seems to be collapsing into rubble at your feet. Or maybe you're having one of those days when life's ordinary frustrations make you feel like a piece of gravel in a cement mixer.

Maybe the best thing to do is to quit trying to tackle the whole thing. Life often is a matter of figuring out how to take a big thing and break it down into smaller parts. I once told a friend how discouraged I was about a writing project I was working on. All I could see was its flaws; each page practically shouted, "I was created by an idiot!" He looked at me gravely and replied, "We all feel that way. But I tell myself that if I'm smart enough to recognize the problems, I'm smart enough to be able to figure out what to do to fix them."

On your MindWalk today, let your feet teach you about perseverance. In taking a walk, what are you doing? You're simply putting one foot after another. Every walk, from a stroll around the block to a trip up Mount Everest, is made up of nothing more than a series of steps, one after another. That accumulation of small steps eventually leads to some form of accomplishment.

We often criticize people for not seeing the "big picture," but sometimes the big picture looks like widescreen Monstervision. That's when we need to learn from watching our feet. Getting started can be intimidating, but rarely will that first step take you right off a cliff. There usually will be plenty of steps ahead in which to adjust your course if you need to. When obstacles appear, as they inevitably will, look for the side paths that let you walk around them.

A teacher once told a class of writing students that if anyone from the class succeeded in becoming a published writer, he or she would not be the most naturally gifted: "It will be the person who refuses to quit. You must always plow on to the end of the row."

Walk on to the end of the row.

Flip Your Attitude

For some of us, it's so easy to get lost in negative thoughts. We pound along, mentally chewing over all the things we've done wrong ourselves like a cow at its cud. Reviewing the seemingly endless list of errors, betrayals, and flops, we are what Joan Didion describes in her magnificent essay on self-respect: "an unwilling audience of one to an interminable documentary that details one's failings, real and imagined, with fresh footage spliced in for every screening."

Sometimes we need to find a way to halt the continuous showing of *I'm Such a Loser*. You might start out on a walk with the movie still playing in your head, but as the same negative thoughts go through their endless loop, use your walk to interrupt them.

One way is what I call "The Flip." When your brain is hammering away at you with criticisms like "Well, you screwed up again" or "You're just too lazy to lose weight," see if there's a way to turn the statement inside out. On your MindWalk today, find something—anything—positive that you can associate with whatever you're beating yourself up over. For example, "Well, I screwed up again" could be countered with "At least I had the courage to try. A lot of people never even give it a shot." The needling about "I'm too lazy" could prompt you to remember a day when you did manage to stick to your diet: "I do have the ability to stick to a diet; I just didn't manage to do it today. But that doesn't mean I never can."

Set yourself the mental challenge of finding a way to flip every negative comment around. If nothing else, thinking about ways to do so can help prevent your thoughts from racing away futilely in the same old gerbil wheel.

Tell yourself, "Flip it."

The Two-Step Mantra

The subconscious is a powerful thing. It can come up with solutions to problems without our realizing it, even while we're doing something else entirely. But it needs a little elbow room in which to work. Our conscious mind is like an elephant in the living room: hard to get rid of and very loud. We need to shut the door on it sometimes. Repeating a simple phrase over and over again has long been used to help focus the mind. In Eastern religions, the repeated phrase or sound is known as a "mantra"; concentrating on humming a sound such as "om" provides a kind of white noise that helps to still the inner chatter of the brain.

I like to use a more energetic variation of this technique when I'm walking, especially if I want to stop obsessing about something. Walking lends itself to using words or phrases with a one-two beat to set up a rhythmic pace. If I'm feeling tired and draggy, I might silently repeat to myself something as simple as "left, right, left, right" as I march along. If I want to pump up my spirits, I might think, "No sweat, no sweat" or "Cour-age … cour-age … cour-age." Other good walking mantras include:

Patience
Help me
Why not?
How come?
So what?

You also could use a four-syllable phrase, such as "You bet I can!" Think the first and third words as your left foot strikes the ground; the second and fourth go with your right. Anything with two or four beats works, and with a little practice you'll find the ones you like best. Somehow, drilling a word like "patience" into the brain by what might seem to be a silly repetition seems to set up a mental pattern that might actually help us be more patient the next time the two-year-old decides to fingerpaint the wall.

Just make sure you do this silently if anyone's around; striding along muttering "So what?" could make you look a little weird. All right, so maybe it's a little weird anyway, but give it a try. By the end of your walk, you just might have a solution to that problem, or remember that nagging errand you keep forgetting.

Do it. Do it. Do it.

100 Wishes

I once went to a seminar in which the leader asked us to close our eyes and visualize where the people in the room who were wearing red were seated. No one knew, of course; we had been concentrating on the seminar topic. The leader then told us to open our eyes, look around the room, and find the people wearing red. It was obviously a much easier task. Because we were actively looking for red, our brains automatically screened out the other colors. The red had been there all along; it was our concentration on it that made the difference.

The speaker's point was that unless we focus on something, it's easily lost among all the things clamoring for our attention. When you're thinking of buying a particular model of car, suddenly it seems that everyone owns one: You see it on every road, in every parking lot, in every driveway. With a mechanism for reminding ourselves what we really want out of life, it's easier to spot ways to make our true desires a reality. I remember reading about a man who at age fifteen listed 100 things he wanted to accomplish before he died. In his seventies, he had crossed off eighty-six of them.

I wish I had had that much foresight. I waited a lot

longer to start my list, which includes everything from taking a weeklong canoe trip to living in the south of France. Though I haven't managed to list 100 goals yet, I'm already a lot closer to achieving some of them than I would have been had I not put my thoughts on paper. I know some of them will change and others will emerge. But for now, if I can accomplish most of what's on my list, my life will have been a pretty good one.

As you walk, begin your mental list of things you want to do before you die: small or large, crazy dreams or projects as down-to-earth as finally getting the basement organized—it doesn't matter. When you get home, put the beginnings of your list on paper. You can add to it whenever you walk. You'll be surprised what long-forgotten plans come to mind when you're forced to come up with 100 wishes. Walking is the perfect time to not only raise your eyes to a new horizon, but to think about how you might pursue ideas that seem utterly unrealistic when you first think of them.

Walk in the direction of your dreams.

A Grateful Heart

In literature the bad characters are often the most interesting. Milton's Satan, the Wicked Witch of the West, Iago—not people you'd want to live with, but not dull. It's the same with life. The bad stuff is in your face all the time, jabbing you in the gut, daring you to forget about it. The good things, on the other hand, get taken for granted. Like the quiet student who sits in the back of the class and always has her homework done, the things for which we should be grateful often get overlooked.

Walks are good for shaking up your thinking. When you find yourself dwelling on whatever is wrong with your life, try a little counteraction. We've talked elsewhere about how walking is a marriage of left and right, a balancing of weight between two points that alternate. You can use the same concept to help lighten whatever burdens you're carrying.

As you walk, imagine a set of scales weighed down with all your problems. Now begin to think of things that could be worse, or that give you a sense of relief. For example, you're out walking; be grateful that you can move under your own power. Many people would be immensely grateful for the chance just to walk as you're doing now. You can be grateful for whatever problems you don't have. As you build a list of life's gifts large and small—the first daffodil of spring, the smile of a small child, the strength you're developing by walking—mentally place each one like a small weight on the opposite end of the scale. You may not be able to get the scale even, but simply reminding yourself of a few of the good things about your life—even if sometimes they're nothing more than an absence of bad—can shift your focus away from the problems that tend to scream for attention.

Let the good child in the back of the room be heard.

The Substitute Buzz

Maybe it's coffee. Maybe it's cigarettes. Maybe it's something more serious that you're trying to cut back on or quit altogether.

Scientists have found that walking helps satisfy many of the same physical cravings that lead people to stimulants. Active movement helps shake off stress, boosts your stamina, clears your mind, gives an exercise high, and zaps the pounds. Sound familiar? They're the same reasons people often give for wanting the buzz of caffeine or one more cigarette.

The next time you find yourself at that point, try substituting a fast ten-minute walk. Studies have shown that ten minutes of walking provide the same sort of immediate lift as caffeine or nicotine, and the beneficial effects last for as long as two hours instead of ten to twenty minutes. Use a MindWalk from the chapter "One Special Thing Each Day" to refocus your mind on the world around you.

If you're feeling strong, substitute some positive imagery. Visualize your body getting rid of the caffeine or nicotine through your pores as you move. Imagine it trailing after you, diminishing in the distance as you leave it behind. See your lungs pumping in fresh air and pumping out tarry residue, or think about caffeine working its way out of your cells to be carried away by the blood that's now circulating like mad. A few minutes —no longer than it would take to go refill the cup or get a cigarette—should help give your body the physical boost it's complaining that it needs.

Walking won't help in situations where you can't get away, and it certainly isn't the sole answer to a craving. But anyone trying to cut back on something knows that every minute is a battle. A walk can provide a momentary distraction. And with more buildings going smoke-free, you may have to head outdoors to smoke anyway.

Why not grab your sneakers and keep on going?

Savor Small Successes

If only we treated ourselves as well as we do our pets. When we're training a puppy, we know that giving it little treats when it behaves well helps it learn good behavior. And yet so often, we don't do the same for ourselves. We may spend so much time thinking about our shortcomings that we overlook the progress we've made.

Walking is one of the easiest ways to create the kind of concrete, measurable achievement that gives the ego the little strokes we all need from time to time. Set yourself a goal—say, walking ten minutes a day. Keep a log in an inexpensive notebook; it can be as simple as making a checkmark on a small calendar for every day you walk your ten minutes. Having a visual record of your progress can help you maintain your program. Watching the checks begin to march in an unbroken line across the page becomes a reward in itself, a visual reminder of what you've achieved. Eventually, you become reluctant to leave a single white space.

I learned the value of savoring small successes when I decided to lose weight after being out of shape for many years. I knew that the most important factor in my program would be to exercise consistently. I wanted to pick something—anything—that I could reliably do every day, just to get myself in the habit. I decided to exercise for five minutes first thing in the morning. I reasoned that no matter how busy I was, I could find time for just five minutes a day.

Sure, I missed a few days, especially at first, but picking an easy target and giving myself visual reinforcement helped me check off most of the days in my first month. I began increasing my exercise time by a minute every day. Becoming consistent about exercise by ramping up gradually was so much easier than trying to go from the sofa to hour-long workouts overnight. Exercise became simply a matter of raising the bar gradually.

If you haven't done this before, set an easy initial goal to achieve, one that lets you succeed fairly easily. If you're trying to walk once a day, make your first goal a walk, no matter how short, every day for a week. At the end of the week, you can set another goal, perhaps walking every day for a month. These small milestones break up an endless future into small, manageable segments, and being able to say, "I did it!" every so often reminds you that the goal is attainable. If you slip occasionally, don't give up; if you have most days checked off, that means you've made progress.

During your walk, picture yourself making your

log entry and feeling a sense of accomplishment. And even though you may be looking at your calendar daily, take a few minutes at the end of a month to review what you've done overall.

Reward yourself for the small victories; over time, they lead to bigger ones.

Leave a Clean Trail

We've talked about scavenging while you walk for things that can make your house more beautiful. But you can also create beauty in another, more public way—by leaving the path cleaner than you found it.

Most serious hikers are careful to leave a trail as they find it by taking out of the woods anything they bring in. I'm talking about going a small step further. I read a magazine article once that interviewed people who made a point of picking up litter as they walked. They carried a small grocery bag and a pair of yard gloves with them. As they walked, they gathered the discarded cigarette wrappers, the empty soda cans, the stray scraps of paper. At the end of the walk, they simply tossed the sack in a trash bin.

Where I live, conservation groups often schedule volunteer cleanup days for the harbor islands. People sign on to spend an afternoon getting rid of human insults to these public parks. You may not have time for this kind of duty—you may feel you do enough cleaning up around the house—but you can accomplish the same effect on a smaller level.

Have I actually done this? You bet. It's not an

everyday occurrence, but I like to do it from time to time as a way to remind myself of just how much waste we all produce. It also leaves the area a bit nicer for my next walk. And as long as I'm careful about how I bend to pick things up—using my legs instead of my waist—the extra squats and bends boost the aerobic value of ordinary walking.

An eco-walk like this can be seen as a gesture of humility, much like early Christians' washing of one another's feet. Leaving your walking routes cleaner than you found them is a profound act of respect for the earth. Think of it as a small prayer for the planet.

A Time to Grieve

When you are in mourning, time seems to stand still. Nothing exists but your grief. Whether the loss is recent or remote, internal or external, you feel like a bell struck by an indifferent hammer whose blow leaves echoes ringing in the ear long after the striking. You know the pain you're feeling will pass eventually, but right now life seems filled with absence.

In this sad time, when your heart is not yet ready to move forward, let your legs move the rest of you. Whether your motion is aimless or purposeful, it is still motion, still a gesture of faith that something still lies ahead. Sorrow relents a bit in the face of simply going on. Think of your walk today as a metaphor for perseverance, for simply getting from Here to There—wherever There winds up being.

As you move through a sepia world like a ghost, your walk becomes a demonstration of the power of persistence. Keep moving until your body has a chance to bathe the brain gently in the biochemicals it manufactures to shield you from stress. You may not have the energy to move fast—indeed, you may not feel you have the energy to move at all—but you don't have to push hard to make the clouds recede a bit. You may not be able to make the pain go away, but moving means that at least you've taken back some small measure of control from a world that seems determined to prove you're at its mercy.

This is what life is about right now: putting foot after foot. There's no need to demand more of yourself —but don't demand less.

Navigating the Terrain

I am not a hiker, but my beloved is. And when we go for what he optimistically calls a "walk in the woods" —which often turns out to be a hike up a steep hill—I am hard-pressed to keep up with those piston legs of his. His Calvinist soul believes you can only enjoy a spectacular view from the top of a mountain if you've exerted a lot of effort to get there. I contend that I can enjoy it just as much if I don't have a veil of sweat dripping off my forehead.

But his trail expertise has taught me a lot. The most valuable lesson came after he followed me down a sharp descent. I was gingerly making my way along the path, afraid that a loose rock would suddenly slip out from under ankles that tend to turn on their sides even on flat ground. Also, as someone who banged up her knees a lot as a kid, I don't entirely trust them now to support me going downhill, especially if I haven't exercised them for a while.

As we picked our way slowly downward, my hiker said, "You're fighting it. Your whole body says that you're afraid of the trail. You've got to let yourself relax and let the trail do its thing. Pay attention to where your feet are going, sure, but let your legs rebound from each footfall like a spring. That way your legs have some give, and the angle at which your foot hits isn't as crucial." He suggested that picking up the pace just a bit might actually increase my comfort level.

He was right. As I began to sink a millimeter or two into each step instead of remaining stiff with fear, I was able to move more quickly. Soon I was practically bouncing down the trail, feeling like a sure-footed little mountain goat.

Walking lets the terrain teach us about life. The road winds. It's rocky. It goes through mud and debris, under trees that have fallen across the path and over stream-slicked rocks ready to dump you on your rear. Sometimes you puff and slog uphill; sometimes you're scared of falling or losing the way. And you don't always know exactly what's at the end.

As you're walking—no matter whether you're on a city street or a mountain trail—remember that sometimes it's best to let your path in life dictate your response. And that relaxing into it, with all its ups and downs, can help you go faster.

Move Toward Your Goals

"If one advances confidently in the direction of his dreams, and endeavors to live the life which he has imagined, he will meet with success unexpected in common hours."

I sometimes think of that wonderful quote from Henry David Thoreau while I'm on a MindWalk. I picture my goal lying somewhere in the distance, like the Emerald City shimmering on the horizon in *The Wizard of Oz*. As I walk, every step I take moves me toward reaching that goal. I begin to think of what I can do to help push my dreams closer to reality: making that phone call I've been putting off, filing that pile of papers so I can find the one newspaper clipping I need to do an assignment. Little by little, these small steps help me advance confidently in the direction of my dreams.

Sometimes the horizon is difficult to see; it may be shrouded in trees or blocked by buildings. As with many projects, the goal lies concealed, the path toward it unclear. When I'm moving toward one of these uncertain ends, I try to focus on the process rather than the outcome. Simply taking one step after another is the equivalent of making a list of tasks and then committing myself to doing only what's on that list. Task by task, I go forward; even though the result may be uncertain, action is better than simply standing in place.

Like a boat moving through water, movement sends out energy. A basic law of physics tells us that for every action, there is an equal and opposite reaction. When you take action, something will happen in reaction. You can't know what that reaction will be, but it may help get you to the point where you can dimly see an outcome in the distance.

As you MindWalk today, move in the direction of your dreams.

MindWalks in
Time and Place

The question is not what you look at, but what you see.
Henry David Thoreau

The First Walk of Spring

It comes first as a gentle breeze that drifts across your cheeks as lightly as a piece of pastel silk. The breeze whispers of flowers that still sleep in curled-tight balls, waiting to be coaxed out so they can put on petticoats of brazen color; of sun that will burst on you like a smile, warming and glazing dry skin in honey-colored light; of a green that hesitates, hinting of richer greens to come. Skies are so newly blue and brilliant that your eyes ache.

The first day of spring comes not by the calendar but with the first day when the weather relents and allows the earth to breathe again. You stretch; you can feel yourself climbing out of your winter skin. Limbs lose their huddled tension, like a woman gradually beginning to trust once again a faithless lover. You want to get outside and move. Energy electrifies your spirit; spring has changed your batteries, stripped off the grime, and set you out gleaming in the sun.

You can't help hearing a lilting Strauss waltz as you walk. You stand straighter, aware of your body moving more freely as you dare to let slip that first layer of winter swaddlings and emerge from your gray winter cocoon. You peel another layer, then another as the day waxes and warms, your body increasingly greedy for bareness until that warmth begins to reverse itself and fades to a cool evening reminder that the best is not here, not yet. Like a lily, spring comes and goes during the course of a day, waiting for a time when it is allowed full run of the earth, when daylight breaks its curfew like an exuberant teenager and stays up late.

Frozen soil softens, preparing to give birth. Its damp smell infuses the mornings as you walk past colors that are as crisp as the snap of a tart apple. White-washed houses stand like clean laundry against a deep blue ocean of sky. Red brick soaks up sun, radiating warmth like a terra cotta oven. Any chill that survives loses its power to abuse.

In spring, the morning of the year, all things are possible. Tarnished plans are rubbed clean and set out anew. Crocuses bloom in your soul.

Summer Abundance

A poet once said that the two most beautiful words in the English language are "summer afternoon." Summer is the season of the senses, the time when living things express most fully what they are. Flowers and vegetables glow with rich color and spill over their baskets at farmers' markets. Trees stretch wide and tall, a million leaves defending the ground beneath them from the sun. We are overwhelmed by the plenty around us, which seems somehow both familiar and new.

Warmth slows life to a calmer pace, softening even the tar on the streets. In summer, limbs stretch lazily. A brief moment of rest on a sofa or in a hammock can drift into a nap, the body melting into loose-limbed languor. Bare legs revel in the sun that pours over them like lotion, and we dress like children again in shorts, T-shirts, and sandals. The sun roasts the sweat out of our bodies. All the world seems to seek out the cool touch of water; we immerse ourselves in it, or trace with our finger a streak in the icy frost on a glass of lemonade. The crisp blast of air conditioning from an open door is a small, momentary oasis off a hot summer street, and stepping indoors feels like entering another dimension.

Instead of hiding until after we are long out of bed, the sun wakes the world with a gentle nudge, urging us to come out to play. There seems to be time enough for everything, though days shrink by invisible seconds as they pass. The perfect summer day is the most delightful of illusions, one that tricks the mind into thinking that life will always be this way. Nature is full and proud, generous in its displays even as it prepares to renege on its promise of abundance.

The world beckons us to exploration, and in doing so we explore ourselves. It is the season for interrupting our routines, for allowing the places we visit to add a new layer to our lives: new family stories, new photos in the album, new relationships, new understandings. Like trees adding a new circle of bark to the concentric rings around its center, we grow.

Savor your MindWalks during this season of warmth; catch every moment of summer before it slips away.

Last Light

Fall arrives with a snap of the fingers and a sharp glance that says, "Pay attention, now!" It snips away at the languor of summer, demanding that we return to grown-up pursuits. One morning we find ourselves fishing longer sleeves out of the closet, and putting socks on feet that never expected to be cold again.

On fall excursions, cheeks redden from the brisk air, and we move a little faster to burn off the chill. Morning walks seem to begin earlier now, though the alarm is set for the same time as always; afternoon walks often end in darkness. The world takes on the warm colors of perpetual sunset, as if the year itself clings to the last slanting rays of light. Cities bristle with newly returned crowds and prepare once again to snub all the quaint little towns and tacky beach resorts with a self-important reminder that the things of significance in this world take place in tall buildings.

Fall is a time of closure. There is a sense that things are being put in order, being tucked in to protect them from what's to come. Dry leaves rustle like an old woman's whisper. No longer can we pretend that good weather will last forever, that there will always be another nice day to get outdoors. Now there is an urgent need to capture a beautiful afternoon as if it were a butterfly, to make every moment count before the darkness descends. Time resumes its tick-tock, driving us to become efficient, to string checkmarks down the long list of things we need and want and have to do.

This season of adjustment gives us a new will to make the most of every hour. Walk in these ever-shorter days of warmth and golden light, and store that energy for the months ahead.

The Dead Time

In the winter air, nothing moves. Under gray skies, time is endless; the earth has paused on its slow path around the sun, and we seem forever caught as we are. Sounds are muffled, movement awkward and slow. Our bodies seek to conserve the warmth inside, to layer our bones with barriers against the cold that slaps our cheeks red. Other animals have wisely hidden themselves to avoid what they cannot master. The world holds its breath, dreaming of a future not yet disclosed.

This is the time for turning inward, for learning to look for the beauty of subtlety and nuance. Winter erases with a firm hand. Harsh gusts of wind wipe the slate clean, making ready for the delicate script of spring. The season's gifts come in a neutral palette: glistening black branches, weathered textures of wood and stone, the glowing light of a distant window set like a jewel in a drift of cotton. Bird tracks stitch a quilt pattern in the snow; human footprints whisper stories of the passage of others. Words emerge into the air and freeze into a brittle shower of stars. Life moves unseen, like water under river ice.

A winter walk is a search for redemption, for laying

frozen offerings of feet and hands and noses on the altar of a universe with a heart of ice. We look forward to home with its welcoming pot of tea, or we sip hot cider from a thermos we have tucked in our pocket. And yet this dead time is the season of the winter solstice, when the days begin gradually to reclaim a few minutes each day from the darkness. When we celebrate the holidays, we celebrate that turning toward the light—a glow reflected in our own generosity of spirit. Walking through this silent time, remember that the light of spring, however distant it may seem, is ahead. For all its stillness, the world is dreaming into being its new life to come.

Walk on, and let this time teach you patience.

A Morning Walk

You're up, you're out before anyone else in the house is awake. As you walk out the front door, the silence of the streets hits you. The day is taking a final snooze before the alarm goes off, drifting in a halfway world between sleep and being fully awake. As you walk along, you revel in being the only person around to see this day fresh. It is still a time of possibilities, unspoiled by conflict or the musts and shoulds and have-tos to come.

The few sounds you notice at this time of day are like no other. Birds rehearse their song, warming up for some unknown performance. Morning mist casts a gray haze like translucent tissue over the landscape before it burns off. As the sun begins to find its way higher, it sneaks through leaves to paint patterns on the ground. Fingers of light creep around corners, creating unexpected shadows that will disappear as the light becomes flatter.

You are alone and can stop to do things without worrying about what anyone around might think. You can sing back to the birds without fear of embarrassment. You can skip or weep or throw imaginary punches at an imaginary enemy. Who is around to care? If you do come upon someone, enjoy the camaraderie of people who know they share the secrets of the morning.

Your soul full of new light, you head home, ready for what will come. You feel energized; your overnight brain has temporarily backed yesterday's problems into a corner. You have stolen some time for yourself, before the world can chain you to tasks and responsibilities.

You've started the day on the right foot—literally.

Noon on Foot

The phone has been ringing nonstop, the dog threw up this morning, and you don't feel so hot either. You've got a presentation tomorrow that you haven't started working on yet, the dry cleaner lost your best suit, and the computer is down—again. And it's only noon.

Time for a walk. Sometimes the only thing that can combat the craziness is a momentary escape. Throw on your walking shoes, and head for the door.

Walking at midday gives you the opportunity to hack off the remaining ragged ends of the morning and start all over again, if not fresh then at least refreshed. It helps you carve the day into more manageable pieces. In the city, faces are everywhere, waiting to have stories invented about them; in the country, the sounds of insects busy at their chores may be your only company.

Feel the light of the sun surround you; too often, those of us who work in offices never see the sun from November through March because work lasts longer than daylight. Studies have shown that a lack of sun hitting the retinas of the eyes is a big factor in the seasonal affective disorder that leaves so many people listless and depressed in winter. As you walk, imagine your eyes drinking in the therapeutic light. Use the opportunity to walk off stress that may have accumulated in your neck and back muscles during the morning. You may feel like taking a brisk hike to relieve tension, or a relaxed saunter to change your mental pace. Brown-bag a lunch in case you find a good spot, or simply find flavor in the walk itself.

At midday, the chance to drop out for a few minutes and regain your perspective can make the difference in whether your afternoon is more of the same. Office walls can begin to feel like they enclose the entire world; so can a home, especially one with small children. It's good to change scenery to remind yourself that there is an entire world that is separate from your current reality.

Let your feet give your brain a rest.

Put a Period to the Day

In the late afternoon, the world begins to hush, like an audience settling down in the moments before the conductor lifts his baton. The light stretches out and gets horizontal in its celestial easy chair. The insistent, twittering phone falls silent; this pulled-thin rubber band of a day goes slack. Muscles begin to believe that they can relax, that maybe for a few hours they won't need to steel themselves against another crisis.

The late afternoon is a time of letting go. When we walk, we are able to put the day in perspective, sort out its twists and turns, untie a few knots. We may have more chores waiting for us when we get home, but we're no longer pushing the day uphill; we're on the downward slope, heading toward rest.

If you're a commuter, the idea of taking a short walk before getting in the car or on the train to head home may sound strange. However, it can help put a period to the run-on sentence of the day. Walking off the day's frustrations before heading home can put you in a more relaxed frame of mind when you arrive. It helps separate work from the rest of your life—something that's increasingly difficult to do as we all become more electronically leashed to the office.

Or walk when you get home, before you get caught up in dinner and bedtime. Walk away from the day, and feel dusk begin to settle around your shoulders like a comfortable shawl. Let your heart and mind take on the stillness that begins to unfold as people retreat into their homes, weary of today but not yet prepared for tomorrow. Let the fading sun pronounce a final benediction as its warm light fades away slowly, silently.

Let your late afternoon walk put today in the past tense.

L'Heure Bleu

The blue hour. It's what the French call the time when the sun has set but darkness has not yet taken over. The day has finally come to terms with its mortality. The white light of noon has been sifted so most colors of the spectrum disappear over the horizon with the sun. Only blue remains to tint everything with a lingering nostalgia, reminding us of old loves. It is the last farewell to color before night, which permits us to see only in black and white.

Lights begin to warm windows. As you pass them on your walk, you get glimpses of unknown lives; you are an audience to a series of ten-second domestic dramas. Flowers begin to close; the green of leaves grows deeper. The bold sounds of day are increasingly muffled, and more intimate sounds emerge: the breathy, rhythmic *skreek* of crickets, the soft pad of your own footsteps. On city streets, people freed from the constraints of work can become their most private selves, or lose themselves in a swirl of others.

The weeds that release a fusillade of pollen during the day cease their fire, and the demonic hacking and sneezing that plague allergy sufferers abate. This last walk two or three hours before bedtime drains off the muscle tension and mental detritus of the day, tiring the body just enough to let it ease more gently into sleep. It's a chance to do some mental sorting and filing of the day's problems, to clean off the inner desktop for tomorrow.

Walk during l'heure bleu, and let the day slip away from you.

Patterns in the Sand

"Whenever it is a damp, drizzly November in my soul ... I account it high time to get to sea as soon as I can," said Herman Melville in *Moby Dick*. Many of us have the same impulse to be near water when we want to think. Walking on the beach seems to soothe the soul in a way nothing else can. There is infinite variety in the combination of wind and sky and sea, in the water's moods, in the tide's new offerings. When all your senses are alive, you could walk on the same beach day after day and yet never truly walk the same beach twice.

If it's a bright day, feel the sun and air on your face as you watch the sun turn the water's surface to diamonds. On a day like this, I often think of those American Impressionist paintings of girls in white dresses facing out to sea, the breeze carelessly tossing their hair. All is light and air and calm; nothing bad can happen on such a day, when nature and body become one. If you're troubled, treasure this walk as a moment of light in the darkness.

Listen to the rhythm of the waves; let them act as an aural massage, gently stroking your psyche clean. On a rocky beach, the stones chutter, chutter, chutter softly to one another as they tumble into the water, dredged seaward by each receding wave. Take a long purifying breath of salt air, inhaling deeply enough to imprint the scent so you can remember it later. The waves may flirt gently with your toes or come barreling in as breakers, translucent in the sun as they curl over themselves to crash in white surf. Whether the sand is a wide, flat sidewalk or loose, shifting dunelets, look at the patterns left by the lapping of the water as you would an abstract painting.

Inspect the ground beneath your feet. A rocky beach holds all sorts of wonders in a patch of seemingly unremarkable pebbles. Spend a few minutes to really examine one of those patches—seeing trees rather than a forest— and I guarantee you'll discover at least one with a striking individual character. Try to find a small treasure that speaks to you with its color or shape: pure white stones, smooth as alabaster; a heart-shaped stone with fiery veins of rust; a smooth, black, fist-sized rock bisected by a streak of quartz. Intact shells are always a joy, but even a shell fragment may contain subtle, wonderful shadings of warm beige and white. Forage for bits of beach glass, whose velvety surface comes from being scrubbed by wave-driven sand.

Even gray days by the water have their own beauty.

The pounding of high surf and the omnipresent sky are potent reminders of the power of nature. They help put our problems in perspective, reminding us of the ebb and flow of life. What is painful and overpowering now is subject to the power of time, the days that follow one after another like wave upon wave. Those days eventually wear away pain as the water sands down the beach glass, the friction rounding its sharp edges and buffing its surface to a powdery softness. Like glass, we too tumble in the breaking waves, and in the turbulence, become more than we were.

St. Augustine said, "It is friction which polishes [us]. It is pressure which refines and makes [us] noble." As you walk by the waves, feel yourself being transformed.

Into the Woods

The silence. The first thing you notice when you enter the woods is the silence. You penetrate beyond the reach of car engines and construction, beyond road and building and machinery, to the point where some sounds —insects, bird calls, a falling branch—become louder because there are no other sounds to muffle them. The occasional noise in the distance serves only to remind you of what you have left behind.

There's a sense in the woods of being welcomed into a secret world where you are surrounded by things more eternal than yourself. Trees overhead are protective; they enclose you like a green cave. You walk as a visitor here. On either side of the path lies the unknown in the underbrush. Plants take shelter beneath other plants. Watchful, motionless animals are betrayed by rustling leaves as they move away from your intruder's footsteps.

A halo of insects sings beside your ears, dances in front of your eyes, swarms onto back and neck and shoulders. They tease you as the Lilliputians did Gulliver, amused that you think any amount of swatting will ever rid you of them. Berries tantalize like rubies and black pearls from beside the path, daring you to pick them; mushrooms of mysterious shapes and colors sprout underfoot. Is any of this treacherous bounty edible? Is it not? You don't know and must walk on, imagining the pioneers who had no choice but to forage and experiment or die. Paths lead off the main trail—or do they? Are they true trails, or mere diversions that lead us only to turn and reverse our steps? Only experience can tell. Civilization's knowledge is useless here; our connections with nature have been weakened, and we no longer know this environment in the core of our being.

Woods walks lead us back to our most primitive selves, before man believed that nature was something to control and manipulate. Away from civilization, that idea seems a fiction. In this place, man is only one part of a very large whole. Walk into the woods, and remember your wild self.

City Sidewalks

In the city, energy crackles all around you. People stream down the sidewalk on a thousand different errands. Buildings surrender to demolition, or swell and adopt new shapes and faces. The rhythms of the city may sound more like jazz than a soothing pastorale, but an urban walk can provide just as much inspiration as a stroll in the woods.

Unexpected sounds drift out of a second-story window—a music student practicing the flute, or a radio with a song that reminds you of when you drove around on summer nights in your parents' car, stalking adventure. A tiny flower struggles through a crack in the sidewalk, offering hope for everyone whose dreams have been paved over. Window displays offer palettes of rich seasonal color, beauty that is free even if the merchandise is not. The scents that steam from sidewalk vendors' carts or the kitchens of nearby restaurants set out a generous buffet for the nose. Architectural details—a stone carving above a door, a white windowsill against a peacock-colored wall, the subtle textures and patterns of brickwork—reveal themselves to those who care to look. No matter how bland the landscape, there is always something new to see when you are observing at a walking pace instead of through the window of a moving car or bus.

Do a little creative eavesdropping. Several years ago I crossed paths with a couple walking toward me and caught just enough of their conversation to make me curious about the story behind it: "She was going to get her Ph.D. in nuclear physics, but then she decided to get it in molecular biology." It left me with an unfinished story, one for which I could choose the ending and invent the main character. This brief scrap from someone else's life also spoke volumes about the university town where I live.

If you prefer solitude, the city in the early morning is yours. Others on the street are also on public retreat; you glance at each other knowing that each has his or her own world to explore before the rest of the day intrudes. Bakeries are opening their doors for early coffee, newspapers at the corner market are still unbundled, the asphalt canyons have not yet filled with light, and rows of residences still shelter their inhabitants. You can examine the city before it wakes up and starts staring back at you with critical eye.

Discover a city on foot.

Country Roads

What is it about the country that attracts us? Is it an ancestral memory of the farmers we all were centuries ago? Or is it simply that time moves more slowly in the country, leaving space to listen to ourselves? A MindWalk down a country road puts us back in touch with an environment that is real rather than designed by man, one with sights and sounds and smells in which marketing executives and space planners had no hand.

Trees arch overhead, forming a sheltering patchwork corridor. In summer, insects are busy running a distant workshop full of tiny table saws. In winter, the cold stills all sound vibrations, like a musician who lays a hand across strummed strings. You walk a silent path, even though an entire world lies in the underbrush a few yards away.

The occasional car may appear and disappear, an intrusive reminder that for the moment, you are of only passing consequence to a world bent on getting somewhere fast. The few houses there are sit quietly back from the road, offering clues to their owners' lives: a child's toys left in the yard, the big metallic bonus-on-wheels that gleams in the driveway, landscaping that shows either careful attention to detail or a submission to nature.

Country roads remind us of the way things used to be, even if they never really were quite the way we imagine. A walk along one of them is a return to things past, to our collective memory of a slower era when we were less linked electronically with other people and more in touch with ourselves. Take the time to live—even if only for the space of this walk—at a country pace.

Hurrah for Blah

When the sky is as gray as lint, it's easy to say, "I don't want to get out in this. I'll wait until the weather's nice." If you do, you'll deny yourself a very special experience. OK, maybe you don't want to go out if it's actually pouring, but try an excursion just after the downpour has stopped. A MindWalk in the rain-slick, wet world has a totally different quality from one in the sun.

Photographers know that a dark, overcast day can paradoxically make colors richer. If you're in a natural environment, leaves becomes nearly fluorescent; set against such deep green intensity, flowers turn into small explosions of color. Gray stones that are otherwise quite ordinary become sleek, seal-like.

Sniff the smells brought out by the newly damp air that soaks into the soil. The clouds seem to hold the world's scent close to the ground rather than letting it dissipate into lighter air. In spring, you may catch the scent of freshly dug earth waiting to mother new plants; in autumn, wood smoke drifts over wet fallen leaves that have the shimmer of enameled gold. Look closely at a raindrop on a leaf. The gleaming curved surface magnifies whatever is underneath, disclosing microscopic secrets.

Are there metaphors for life here, to help us through our own overcast days? The old cliché about "into each life some rain must fall" doesn't capture the way that the dark times also illuminate. The days when sorrow storms our souls can intensify the joy of those that are pure sunshine. Our battles can bring out unexpected wonder: new friends, hidden resources. We don't know what rich colors we're capable of producing until stormy weather brings them out.

On your rainy-day walk, think of whatever is casting black shadows over your life—and how you might be able to use the darkness to produce a more intense life, with colors so bright they burn.

Meet You at the Mall

Many people walk in malls: They're convenient, sheltered from the weather, secure from street hazards, and they offer level surfaces. They're perfect for an exercise program. Trouble is, they can be a little too perfect. Without the kind of variables that walking outdoors offers, mall walking may get dull after a while unless you're with a friend. Many malls sponsor group walking programs, but you can also MindWalk.

A friend of mine contends that everyone in New York has an interesting face—not necessarily a beautiful face, but an interesting face. Whenever I visited the city, I used to test his theory and realized he was right. Each face I looked at had at least one element that hinted at some sort of story behind it. Viewed with the right attitude, each unique combination of nose, eyes, mouth, cheeks, chin, ears, forehead, and hair is the product of a life, of parents' and grandparents' lives, and of a cultural heritage.

Take a good look around you the next time you hit the mall for shopping or exercise walking. Interesting faces aren't exclusive to New York. Glance discreetly at individuals and push yourself to notice what's remarkable about each one. Try to imagine what has led that person to this point in his or her life.

Another way to liven up mall walking is to select a remote destination and find out the mileage from where you live. Pick somewhere you've always wanted to go—for me, it would be Santa Fe—or a place you've been to and loved. Then keep a log of how far you've walked each day—simply jotting it on a calendar will do—so you can track roughly where you are on your journey. Imagine the scenery as you walk across the Rockies on your way to California, or down the road that strings together the Florida Keys.

Mall walking doesn't have to be boring. It's all a question of where your mind is.

Walk with the Animals

We walk with animals every day. We're surrounded by two-leggeds and four-leggeds whenever we walk down a city street. One of the pleasures of walking is coming across tiny wildlife unexpectedly: a lizard on a fencepost, a bird that is nothing more than a brief flash of plumage. But for a change of pace, a stroll around your local zoo can reintroduce you to a theater of sights and sounds you would otherwise have to imagine or travel to see.

Some zoos around the country hold regular zoo walks, introducing visitors to the characters within their walls. Thankfully, many zoos have moved away from cages and wherever they can, have put animals in their natural habitats and larger spaces more enjoyable for both beast and observer. Whether self-guided or in a group, a zoo walk is probably longer on entertainment than on exercise, but strolling around among fellow animals with less freedom also can remind us of how we take for granted the ability simply to be mobile, to wander as we please.

As you stroll, look for lessons about our own animal behavior. With a little imagination, you can spot someone you know. See the monkey taunting his companions like a six-year-old? Look at the hippo wallowing sleepily in a sun-warmed pond the way you love to lie in a hammock on summer Sundays. Watch the lions move with controlled strength as they eye the crowd suspiciously, predators waiting for the next corporate takeover.

Get out of your lair, and remind yourself of your animal nature.

WALKS WITH COMPANIONS, WALKS IN SOLITUDE

*I have met with but one or two persons in the course
of my life who understood the art of Walking …
who had a genius, so to speak, for sauntering.*

HENRY DAVID THOREAU

Let the River Flow

Y ou cannot step twice into the same river," said the
Greek philosopher Heraclitus. He meant that
nothing remains the same from moment to moment.
We are like sticks standing upright in the river, he said;
even if we stay still, the river flows on around us, constantly changing our surroundings. But there are times
during a MindWalk when I am able to feel the stillness
more than the rush of activity. I imagine myself as that
stick thrust into the river: calm and centered amid
everything that ebbs and swirls around me. Meditators
call it "being in the moment": being fully present in
whatever you are doing.

Just for this moment, you are grounded, stable, balanced within yourself; everything else is fluid, subject to
change. The nagging inner voice is silenced. You're not
distracted by thoughts of where the stream has come
from and where it's headed. For this moment, you need
only be, not do. However temporarily, you are not a
worker, a parent, a spouse. You are simply a being at
rest, conscious of itself as separate from the rest of the
world even as you move through it.

Erasing the world is easier if you concentrate

intently on something. Meditation teaches us to focus on breathing; doing so puts our attention within our bodies and lets it ride gently on the rhythm of the air going slowly in and out. Close examination of the drifting clouds, a small exquisite flower, an intricate pattern of tree limbs can also place us in the moment.

On your walk, find a safe place to stop and take a break from the world. Close your eyes if you feel comfortable doing so. Taking a deep, slow breath helps draw a line between this moment and the flow of time. And when you decide to move on, let your walk keep you outside the minutes that tick by.

There will be time enough to let the river carry you onward when you return.

Head for the Door

There's nothing easier to postpone than confronting conflict. There never seems to be enough time, or the right kind of time. A drive in the car may throw people together on the way to something else, but unless it's a long trip, it may not encourage intimacy. And if there's tension in the air, conversation may shut down completely or, worse, set off an argument.

Walking can create a good setting for addressing conflict. It's cheap, it's convenient, and it doesn't get you where you're going so fast that it makes conversation perfunctory. Somehow you find yourself talking about things that seem to get neglected in the ordinary course of the day. Walking creates a connection; you're literally in step with each other.

As pleasurable as walking can be when two people are feeling close, it can be even more beneficial if conversation is strained. A contradiction? Hardly. Maybe you've wanted to talk about something but can't quite figure out how to bring it up. Or maybe there's simply an undercurrent of tension that needs to be dispelled (the socks got left on the bathroom floor *again*).

Walking while you talk things out can help in a

couple of ways. Striding along channels the tension in your body into productive exercise rather than destructive words; you're walking off the anger. Second, a change in the focus of your attention—both people looking straight ahead—can make it easier to discuss a subject that might cause confrontation if you were sitting face-to-face. The sounds and sensations of the outdoors help fill in the anxious gaps between sentences. Sitting around the kitchen table or across a desk, it's too easy to stumble into saying the wrong thing simply to fill the cavernous silences. And you're away from the distractions—TV, kids, chores, the phone—that make it easier to let problems lie like sleeping dogs waiting to wake up and bite.

Next time you have something uncomfortable to talk about, head for the door.

Walk Hand-in-Hand

It seems like such a simple gesture. One hand clasps the hand of another as you walk with the person you love. And yet research has shown that holding hands not only expresses an emotional bond between two people; it actually helps create that bond.

When you walk hand-in-hand, you are in the world, and yet there is also a world that exists only between the two of you. You move apart and then together again, always linked by touch. It is as if the vein that the Romans thought connected the heart to the fourth finger of the left hand simply kept on going out the end of your fingertip, flowing directly into the vein of your partner.

Walking with a loved one can help you stick to an exercise program, but there's also something to be said for the occasional walk that benefits the heart in other ways. It's an opportunity to defuse tensions with the touch of a hand, to be more reflective than you otherwise might in the ordinary course of a day. Let a simple squeeze, palm to palm, say things you can't. Let your pace fall into a shared rhythm, a double expression of a single movement. For a time, let the two of you forget everything outside this shared world—kids, work, home

—and enjoy being in the present moment. Remember that the hand you hold is the same hand you held when you first met, a hand you could probably recognize from a thousand others. Walk back in time, even for a moment, to when you were still new to each other's quirks and habits.

Renew your connection as you walk. The power is in your hands.

A Nose for the New

I used to walk with the most enthusiastic of small beagles. Rotier had been through doggie obedience school a couple of times; he was one of those students that gets a passing grade so the teacher can get rid of him. He knew all the right moves, but whenever he was outside, his mind simply got taken over by his hunting-dog nose. I'm not sure there's anything in the world that makes me as visibly ecstatic as being outdoors made Rotier. Hyperobservant (not to mention simply hyper), he strained to get to the next incredible smell, the next amazing patch of grass.

Walking with a pet, like being with a child, can teach us about the wonder that is out there in the world. If we could only enjoy a tenth of what our pets sense, we probably would be overwhelmed at the richness of the everyday. Watch their delight in every encounter, even with something you know for a fact they have seen a hundred times. Every muscle is alert, ready for the new adventure found in every spot-check of bush or curb.

Walking with an eager pet can help keep you moving at a pace that's good for both of you, and an unlocking leash allows some freedom for him and a reminder from you when necessary. If you don't have a pet of your own, call the humane society in your town; some allow volunteers to sign pups out of the pound for a brief furlough.

And while you're walking, try to find something that makes your own mental tail wag. Imagine your nose is as powerful as your pet's and your hearing as keen. You'll be surprised at the new worlds your senses can discover when your pet takes you for a walk.

Home for the Holidays

Holiday celebrations can be treacherous. Family members spend more time than usual around one another, and unspoken expectations of harmony are never higher. Frequently, there are a lot of people in a house with too little to do. The kitchen may be a hive of activity, but not everyone can—or wants to—help with cooking. All too often, new conflicts emerge to join long-simmering ones in a scalding stew. Many times, the holidays have shuttered the activities and places that might siphon off some tensions by getting at least some people out from underfoot.

Rather than sitting around the house waiting for someone to say the wrong thing, why not take a family walk? It's a great way to get rid of the lassitude that often follows a big meal. If frictions arise, it's often easier to tackle difficult subjects when you're walking. You aren't in a face-to-face, confrontational posture but side-by-side, where a sardonic curl of the lip or a skeptical look is less likely to be noticed and provoke angry dialogue. Restless children who might otherwise create havoc can discharge a lot of that energy outdoors; the pace of a group stroll can also create a quiet, reflective mood. The sound of shuffling feet helps fill any awkward silences.

And if everyone's on good terms, a family walk can also be a way to relish that closeness and contemplate the true nature of the holiday. A child's graduation might prompt recollections of peak moments from his or her childhood. If it's Thanksgiving, individual reflections on what there is to be thankful for can be a great walking conversation. Encourage participation in the group walk, but don't draft anyone who really doesn't want to go; you may bring on the very conflicts you want to minimize.

A holiday walk won't solve long-standing family problems. But if holidays and family get-togethers are difficult for you, it's better to walk than to sit around waiting for the time bomb to go off.

Neighborhood Watch

We are so pressed for time now that walking around the neighborhood may be the only way we get to know the people who live near us. Front yards can be a series of small dioramas that say something about the personalities of the people who live there.

If you don't know your neighbors, you're free to invent your own images of them from the clues on display. Even in the blandest of tract developments, where house replicates house like so many photocopies, human nature finds a way to assert its individuality. Do the people with all the Halloween decorations have kids, or are they just kids at heart? Is the small religious shrine in the side yard a memorial to a loved one? Does an unkempt lawn in front of a mansion indicate financial problems? A trip? Sloth?

If you do know your neighbors, your walks may be even more valuable. Citizens in many communities have started neighborhood watch programs. You can do sentry duty as you walk by keeping an eye on the house of someone you know is on vacation. We may no longer wave to passersby from our front porches, but we can still look out for one another.

Vacation Close to Home

When the world seems drab, when even your daily walks don't do for you what they used to, maybe an afternoon walking vacation is what's needed. Set aside several hours—two or three at least—for an extended MindWalk. Go someplace that lends itself to meditation, even if it means driving for a bit. This isn't just an exercise walk, although you definitely will be doing your body a favor. This is time out for the spirit, a cheap, fast way to really put some distance between yourself and the day-to-day. Preferably, you'll be spending some time in a natural setting, but don't feel you have to pick a challenging trail; in fact, you'll probably want an area that encourages you to sit periodically for a while to simply contemplate your surroundings.

If you're time-constrained (and who isn't?), pick a place that's close enough so you don't spend half your time driving to get to it. The idea is to make this a fast, easy vacation, one that can be done without a lot of arrangements in advance. Allow time on the way to pick up some treats small enough to tuck into your pockets or a fanny pack—an ultraluxurious candy bar, a wedge of Stilton, and a cluster of perfect grapes, maybe even a small bottle of wine. They should be special enough to remind you that this is a vacation walk, an escape from the ordinary. If you have a book that can be carried easily, you could also take it along (no textbooks or work related reading, though; you're on a vacation, after all).

When you reach your starting point, take several deep, slow breaths and stretch a few times before starting out. Both can draw a line of demarcation between daily life and your mini-vacation, and give the sense of getting away that an airline flight or long car ride offers. As you walk, open your senses and take in your surroundings, using some of the MindWalks techniques you've learned. Walk until you feel like stopping; start again when you feel like it. Mixing a brisk pace with a more relaxed, exploratory saunter is nice, but this is your vacation to enjoy as you please. Just don't forget to time yourself and turn around halfway through so the second half of the trip won't wind up being longer than you're prepared for.

Taking a walk that's a bit longer than your usual route, that challenges without exhausting, that shows you something new, can be the quickest, cheapest vacation you'll ever take.

Listen to Yourself

Have you ever seen someone whose eyes don't match the face? I don't mean that the person is unattractive or funny-looking. I'm talking about people who smile with their mouths but have eyes as cold and empty as a windowpane in winter, people whose mouths talk to you but whose eyes are constantly on the move around the room to see who else is there. I think of them as people who spend too much time talking with others and not enough time talking with—and listening to—themselves.

With all the demands on us, it's difficult to find time to be alone with ourselves. And yet if we want our brains to be connected to our hearts, if our eyes are to truly engage and be engaged with others, we must have intervals of solitude. We need time to reconnect with what we are feeling, time to simply be ourselves rather than someone's parent or spouse or employee. Time away from noise and demands and interruptions, from the tyranny of things undone.

I walk in part to set aside some time with myself, as I would with a good friend. I like to hear what's been going on with me and how I feel—or would have felt if

I'd had the time to stop and feel anything. Walks give me an outlet for anger, a silent time for meditation, a pause in the day that is something for myself alone. I do many things for many people all day; I also need a little attention. Finding one thing that makes each walk worthwhile—whether it's a sight or thought or sound—guarantees that no matter how bad the day is, at least one thing has brought me joy.

Walking in the morning helps me plan my day, giving it the balance that comes from making sure my focus is on what's truly important. Walking in the afternoon is a welcome break from the pressure of work. Evening walks let me absorb and sift through the events of the day. I reflect on what I could do differently, celebrate the day's small victories, and vent frustrations that could otherwise spoil sleep.

As you walk today, gradually hear your heart's song ever clearer, ever stronger, a solo voice emerging pure and welcome to ears grown dull from not listening closely enough.

NOURISHING
YOUR SPIRIT

*I only went out for a walk, and finally concluded
to stay out till sundown, for going out, I found,
was really going in.*

JOHN MUIR

The Heart Opening

You've been walking for, say, fifteen or twenty minutes. Maybe you're turning over a problem in your mind. Or maybe you're not thinking about anything at all but simply want to get some exercise.

Suddenly you realize that your mental state has undergone a subtle shift. You're less connected to daily concerns, more in tune with your senses and your innermost thoughts. Time seems to blur, thrown out of focus by the sensation of movement. The change happens stealthily in the background of your mind, unnoticed until for no apparent reason you suddenly become conscious of your altered state. You have left the outside world behind and are intensely involved with what's going on inside. It's not an out-of-body experience, but it's not the same frame of mind you have sitting at your desk, either.

Science tells us this almost trance-like state is caused by the rush of endorphins that we've mentioned before. But I prefer the term that practitioners of meditation use for the point of entrance into a different mental dimension: the heart opening. It's as if your innermost being suddenly develops a clear view of things, a communication with a power beyond yourself. Whether that power is a deity or simply the wonder of the world around you, it represents a moment of union between the individual and the universal. Creative thoughts and new solutions surface, much as they do when we sleep and our minds are free to dream unfettered by logic.

Empty your mind, relax into your walk. Like a timid guest, the moment of heart opening will emerge and tap at the door of your consciousness when it's ready.

The Imaginary Conversation

I have a friend to whom I talk maybe once a year. We both care deeply about each other, but we live far apart, both of us have crazy schedules, and it's difficult to get together except as disembodied voices on the answering machine. And yet I have a lot of conversations with her that she doesn't even know about. I talk with her as I'm walking.

Walking with a friend creates an intimacy that lends itself to talking about feelings, hopes, dreams, and fears as much as day-to-day commonplaces. Too often, phone calls and e-mails are simply recitations of what's happened since the last time you talked; they're driven by events rather than thoughts. Like writing a letter, a walking conversation often exposes more of a person's core.

If you're lucky enough to have a walking partner, you know how this kind of sharing can make exercise more enjoyable. If you can't get together, a walk alone is better than none; after all, one reason many people walk is because they can do so on their own schedule instead of being tied to someone else's. But I would give anything to be able to take real walks with my friend of twenty years. When I find myself missing her wisdom and thoughtful advice and can't reach her, I sometimes carry on a silent, imaginary conversation with her as I walk. I may tell her about what's been going on in my life. If I'm worried about something, I try to describe the problem as clearly as possible to her. I imagine what clarifying questions she would ask, what common-sense analysis she would offer. In the process, I often discover new aspects to the situation, or solutions I hadn't thought of before.

In some cases, she reminds me that my problems aren't the end of the world. Sometimes she pushes me to demand more of myself. Sometimes she merely listens and sympathizes.

Imaginary childhood friendships are expected to disappear with adolescence. But in an age of here-today-gone-tomorrow friendships, when even the closest of buddies have to work to find time for each other, sometimes a mental clone of a live person has to substitute temporarily. When I told my mom about my virtual chats, I was surprised to find that she has a mental conversation with her mother—dead for many years—each night before she falls asleep.

If someone has a place in your heart, why not let her accompany you when you walk—even if she's miles away?

Coming Full Circle

"Things fall apart; the center cannot hold," wrote poet William Butler Yeats. Sounds like our lives at times. When family, friends, job, and appliances all seem to conspire to make the day a misery, we need to create for ourselves, to borrow a phrase from another poet, a "still point of the turning world."

This might be the time to take a cue from an ancient meditative practice known as labyrinth walking. A labyrinth offers a structured, contemplative walk that turns the mind inward. Organized around a central point, the path of a labyrinth leads in a spiral or mazelike formation toward that center and then back out, with no dead ends to distract you. It can be seen as a metaphor for the soul's journey through life, death, and rebirth

In medieval times, people who could not make long pilgrimages would walk a labyrinth as a symbolic gesture of devotion. The concept was given new life by Rev. Dr. Lauren Artress of San Francisco's Grace Cathedral in her book *Walking a Sacred Path*. Because of the labyrinth's meditative quality, many churches around the country, like Grace Cathedral, have developed them as devices for spiritual renewal. Like chanting or prayer, walking a labyrinth causes external stimuli to give way to intense concentration on a calming, repetitive rhythm. If you can't find a labyrinth near you, create your own by drawing a spiral in the sand or marking a path with small stones. If done unobtrusively, it may remain your secret.

When you walk a labyrinth, move slowly, deliberately. Imagine giving yourself up to the discipline of the path before you. Just for this moment, no decisions are required of you; there are no mistakes to be made. You need only put one foot in front of the other.

As you move toward the center of the labyrinth, visualize yourself gradually drawing closer to the core of your being. Once in the center, close your eyes, take a deep breath and exhale. Feel that core self radiating from your heart to the tips of your fingers and toes, unifying body and spirit. At the midpoint, you become centered, still.

Whenever you're ready, reverse your steps and walk gradually outward again. Think of taking away with you the stillness you found in the labyrinth's center. You are coming—literally—full circle.

It is rare in life for our path to be clearly defined, to be able to see what lies ahead. By slowly, quietly making your small pilgrimage in a labyrinth, you can enjoy a brief moment of certainty in an uncertain world.

Walk in Sacred Time

Time is relative to the way in which you spend it. Three hours of doing something you enjoy seems like fifteen minutes; fifteen minutes of doing something you hate seem like three hours. All time is not the same.

Someone once outlined the difference between the time marked by clocks and calendars, and sacred time. Clock time is left-brained; sacred time is right-brained. Clock time is what the world runs on; it is concrete, it has definition and limits. Sacred time is what our souls run on; it is limitless and endless. In sacred time, the soul dwells in a separate reality that transcends the tick-tock of life; it is time spent in the Eternal rather than on day-to-day concerns. Clock time has to do with the human, the tangible world. Sacred time is the realm of ritual, of the intangible, the divine; in it, we become one with something beyond ourselves. Meditation, trances, prayer—all are attempts to move from clock time to sacred time for a while, to "stop the clock" and be reunited with that higher existence.

Activities you enjoy also help you connect with sacred time. You feel it when you get involved with a hobby and look up to find that hours have passed without your realizing it. Like taking off a watch, getting deeply involved with what you're doing—being fully present in the moment—is a way of creating a space of sacred time and leaving behind the workaday worries. Losing yourself in your surroundings as you walk, really tuning in to what is around you, also can move you from clock time to sacred time.

When you inhabit sacred time, walking becomes a religious, spiritual activity, a way of worship that takes you beyond yourself. And with all the demands of modern life, time spent out of time is more needed than ever.

Walk today, and create some sacred time for yourself.

Living Whole

I drive my family crazy when we play Scrabble. We're very loose about the rules; for example, we allow a player to check on a word before he or she lays it down. But whenever something exotic—a word like "oe" or "ai"—gets played, I always want to know what it means. It's not that I doubt the word; for one thing, the person playing it is usually sitting there with the open dictionary. I'm just curious.

During one of these dictionary detours, I happened to glance at the word "integrity." There was, of course, the definition we most often think of: "firm adherence to a code of moral or artistic values." But there was also "the quality or state of being complete or undivided."

This reminder came at a time when I had done something, as most of us do at least once in our lives, of which I was not proud. It was the kind of petty betrayal that may not make headlines but that tends to snap the mind awake at 3 a.m. and set it adrift in a sea of guilt. Lying there, what I feared most was not the consequences of the act itself; it would probably never be discovered. It was the recognition that I would always be vulnerable to waking up like this, with the knowledge that I was not the person I had held myself to be.

Seeing that dictionary definition made me start thinking about what it means to have integrity, to be whole. It is not simply a matter of "doing the right thing" in the conventional sense, of following the rules on the top of the Scrabble box or cleaning underneath the bed even though no one will see. It is a matter of heeding that still, small voice that can see the future, that measures the possible outcomes of our actions and sends up a warning cry that we ignore at our peril. It means doing only what we can live with later. The voice instinctively knows what can come of our actions, but many times we stuff a sock in its mouth. But listened to, it can help conquer the tyranny of what seemed like a good idea at the time.

Having integrity does not mean we never do things that can have disastrous outcomes, or that we never take risks. It just means that we have entered into the transaction fully informed about the possibility for disaster and willing to live with whatever comes of our choice. We are not saying one thing and then doing another because our minds are not in sync with our hearts, or our bodies scornful of our minds. We have listened to the voice from the abyss and are prepared to face it if we decide to go over the edge. If our bodies push us to Dionysiac excess, integrity means being willing to accept the next morning's hangover; if we sleep in every morning instead of getting out for a walk, we do not then expect weight to disappear as if by magic. Having integrity means recognizing that B follows A, that risk means the possibility that the enterprise will fail.

Being whole does not ward off random shots from a hostile universe. It does mean that we have recognized in advance that the bolt of bad luck is part of the package we're handed along with our birth certificate. The universe can always sabotage our plans; what can be averted by living whole are the savage reprisals of what we knew all along to be true.

We think of someone who takes a fearless, forthright stand for right and think, "Ooooh, she has such integrity." This kind of behavior gives us a merit badge that everyone can see and admire. Integrity is more difficult to hang on to in the dark places where no one will know but ourselves. Like a flashlight in a dark room, our souls will always seek out and find that hidden flaw, leaving us awake at 3 a.m. to contemplate the spidery recesses of our conscience.

Lacking integrity, we find ourselves in strange beds or strange conversations, listening to things come out of our mouths that have no connection with who we really are. We lie vulnerable, exposed to constant recriminations from that harshest of critics: ourselves.

As you walk today, think of your body moving in harmony with your soul, of all parts of you supporting and extending one another. Let your resources be directed in a unified way against whatever challenges you. Live in an integrated way. Live whole.

The Art of the Saunter

I used to live within driving distance of Key West, Florida. Whenever I went there to visit, time seemed to flow like molasses. Perhaps it was the heat, or maybe the Caribbean sense of time as a plastic concept, something to be molded around experience. Whatever the cause, I found my normally brisk walking pace immediately turned into a slow amble. I learned to choose my walking path by which side of the street had the most shade. In short, I sauntered.

Walking for exercise is restorative, but so is a good saunter. Henry David Thoreau, an avid walker himself, speculates that the word was derived from the name for people who roamed the French countryside in the Middle Ages, asking for alms so they could go to "la Sainte Terre"—the Holy Land. Regardless of whether the pilgrimage ever got made, such a beggar became known as a "Sainte-Terrer," which evolved into "saunterer."

Another possible origin of "saunter," according to Thoreau, is the phrase "sans terre," meaning "without land." Saunterers have "no particular home, but [are] equally at home everywhere." This, he says, is the secret to successful sauntering: to become, at least temporarily, one with whatever landscape surrounds you.

Both meanings work for me. Sauntering indeed brings us to a kind of Holy Land. Taking the time to move deliberately, we discover things that might be missed at a faster pace. And MindWalks are one way to make ourselves at home everywhere, free of roles and responsibilities. With them, we can reclaim the inner landscape that is truly ours, the self we often neglect and to which we must remind ourselves to return.

Whether as an attempt to reach a sacred state or an exploration of emotional territory, sauntering is a pilgrimage of the soul. Go on your journey today—and don't be in too big a hurry to arrive.

Shape the Negative Space

When I took a design class several years ago, our first assignment involved creating patterns by cutting abstract shapes from black paper and placing them against a white background. The only rule was that each black piece of paper had to touch at least one other black piece. When we were finished, the teacher told us to look not at the black design we had laid out but at the white shapes around it, created by the negative spaces between the black paper. It's a variation on the old visual puzzle in which a picture of a vase seems to reverse and become two faces in silhouette.

Think of a MindWalk as that negative space between all the commotion that fills the rest of your day. A MindWalk gives you the chance to carve meaning from the space that surrounds the appointments, the phone calls, the household chores. For most of us, there's not much of that space: all the more reason to try to bring a better balance between foreground activity and background relief, and to make sure that even the few minutes we may have for walking get shaped in a pleasing way.

Walking requires no decisions, no effort beyond

movement. It is simplicity itself. But like the white spaces between the black paper, it can become whatever we make of it.

Get Real

As a species, we have succeeded all too well in mastering our environment. The pioneers who gave us the ability to communicate with one another regardless of distance—the road-builders, the tele-inventors—also constructed a most elegantly designed and attractive trap. Our experiences are increasingly shaped and constructed and ordered, so that we begin to automatically reject the unstructured, the messy, the unexpected. We spend most of our lives meeting arbitrary deadlines in artificial environments where the temperature is constant and controlled. We talk to people through machines; at night we listen to artificial people who live in a little electronic box in the living room. We have mastered our world only to find that it has mastered us.

Walking can take us away, however momentarily, from shaped experience and bring us back in touch with what is real. Even in a city, where man has squared off the curves of nature and put things at right angles, walking lets us weave our own path and open ourselves to whatever the universe may choose to put in it. Fleeting encounters with others—the purchase of a newspaper, perhaps—involve no obligation, no gain or loss on either side; we are free to be ourselves with people who don't care who we are. We experience the world directly rather than filtered through someone else; we see things with our own eyes, hear with our own ears.

When we walk, nature has the upper hand, not man. We get hot or feel the wind on our faces. Plants find ways to escape any designated boundaries; they push through sidewalks, sneak over and around fences. However momentarily, where we go is in our own hands, and we live our own lives instead of someone else's version of them.

As you MindWalk today, rejoice in this escape to reality.

Elude the Body Snatchers

I had a friend once, a single mother of two, who declared to her children that once they graduated from high school, they were on their own. "Right now it's my turn to be Mom," she told them, "but once you're old enough to take care of yourselves, I get to be Joanne again."

Sometimes life feels like a variation on the classic science fiction movie *Invasion of the Body Snatchers*. Because of all the daily demands on our time, our hearts, our minds, it feels as though someone has stolen our selves and replaced them with meal-making, report-writing, grocery-shopping, car-driving, phone-answering automatons. Too often we lose ourselves in what must be done for our bodies and our families to survive, in the process, we forget what must be done for our souls to survive as well.

Sometimes on a walk, it's enough simply to revel in having a brief time away from everything and everyone. The only decision you have to make is which route you want to follow; the only questions you have to answer are the ones you ask yourself. Silence is a gift from the universe, allowing you to reclaim yourself from the bodysnatchers, however well-meaning and beloved they may be.

As you MindWalk today, rejoice in doing something just for yourself.

Prime the Pump

Have you ever seen someone prime an old-fashioned water pump? It takes a few vigorous shoves on the handle to get the water moving upward until it finally reaches the spout and is driven out in rhythmic, synchronized gushes.

Walking primes the pump, physically and mentally. You might start out sluggish and exhausted, but after you've been out a few minutes, you can feel the stream beginning to flow. Oxygen wakes up the brain; the blood begins to circulate through every part of the body, surging into the cells and gently washing away the waste they no longer need. You can practically feel it moving through you, flushing your cheeks, pushing sweat out the pores as if your skin were a giant radiator. When you stop for a moment, you feel your heart for the mechanism it is, the insistent engine that powers the pump.

If you're upset about something, imagine this physical refreshing as an emotional cleansing, too. Walking helps drain off the anxiety and pain that too often poison the system and close you off from the world. Just as the heart sends blood to the cells to nourish and replenish them, picture it pumping waves of healing through the psyche to calm, soothe, and comfort. The faithful heart floods the body and mind with fresh life, which carries away in its ebb what is not wanted. Getting rid of all that sludge—physical and emotional—prepares you for renewal.

Prime the pump today.

Walk a New Path

If you've been walking regularly, chances are you have a set routine, a route you travel more often than not. It's wonderful to watch the way the seasons or the time of day can work magic on familiar sights; seeing the new in the everyday is a big part of what MindWalks are all about. But taking an unaccustomed path, or a detour on an accustomed one, can bring experiences you can't anticipate. Serendipity—the spontaneous appearance of unexpected pleasures—is a powerful force. We learn most from exposure to new things. They broaden our perceptions, give our psyches a new backdrop against which to set existing attitudes, beliefs, and feelings.

Sometime it takes courage and imagination to attempt the new; by definition, we will have to cope with situations for which we do not feel well-equipped. We do not necessarily know the end result or what we may encounter along the way; that uncertainty is what makes many of us stick to the path we know. But every so often we need to flex the psychic muscles we use to deal with the unfamiliar. After all, life itself is a big unknown. If we don't exercise those muscles they get weak, and we're unable to cope when we need them most: when life throws us those big curve balls.

I remember one day I decided to take a slight detour from my favorite walking trail through the park, which ran along a river. I knew there was a parallel path that ran along the river's opposite bank, but in all the walks I had taken by the water's edge, I had never tried the other way. It was a beautiful spring day; new growth was everywhere on the trees around me. The air was full of promise. I decided to cross the river and walk back home on the other side.

The new path turned out to be nothing more than a narrow dirt track that wound through the woods. As I walked along in my sneakers, it became muddier, more narrow; there were large patches where the sun hadn't yet reached and ice still clung to the ground, making walking more treacherous than I had expected. I found myself clambering over rocks, stretching precariously to cross small ravines. This was hiking, not walking, and I worried about what would happen if I, walking by myself in an area by now relatively deserted, fell and could not get home.

Yet I remember that walk now as one of my most treasured. I saw waterfalls still frozen in mid-cascade down the gray stone hills. I got a helping hand across a treacherous ice slick from a couple who had passed me earlier and turned back to make sure I was OK crossing the ravine. I got a much better workout from all the clambering I was forced to do. And I felt a sense of achievement, of conquest, that I would not have had if I had stuck to the path I knew.

I'm not advocating recklessness; the unknown can have disastrous consequences. But even when things don't work out well, there are valuable life lessons in the mistakes. Nature is a wonderful conservationist; nothing is wasted.

Try a new path today.

Free to Be

There is a wonderful moment in the children's story of *Pinocchio* when the puppet realizes he is no longer tied by strings to someone who controls his every move. At last, he moves not with a jerky, disjointed gait manipulated from above, but with an easy, confident stride that says, "I can go anywhere I want."

With all the demands on us, it's easy to feel like a puppet ourselves, twitched this way and that at the whim of others. A child pulls the Mom string and our limbs clatter to attention. The Spouse string tugs and our feet move toward the kitchen or laundry. One jerk on the Worker string, and we shuffle out of bed and off to the office.

As you MindWalk today, envision yourself transformed like Pinocchio. The web of tangled strings drops off; you are free to move unencumbered. Shake your wrists to untie the threads of responsibility that manipulate you. Feel your muscles controlling your body rather than letting it move automatically, a passive collection of linked bones. As you walk, let yourself become more human and less the puppet person that the world often demands.

If you don't like the Pinocchio image, maybe Gulliver is more suitable; in the land of the Lilliputians, he found himself roped to the ground, the strings pulled tight by tiny tormentors. Either way, imagine breaking loose—at least momentarily—from the day-to-day constraints that frustrate, hamper, and impede you, leaving you feeling helpless.

Walking lets you cut the strings for a brief time and simply be.

Close the Loop

There's a passage in T.S. Eliot's *Four Quartets* that I've always liked:

We shall not cease from exploration
And the end of all our exploring
Will be to arrive where we started
And know the place for the first time.

It speaks to me of our ability to discover ourselves by pushing a bit further than is strictly necessary. I once made a job change that required moving away from the place where I had spent most of my adult life, a place I loved but that had become too familiar, too predictable. I was ready for a change—or so I thought. The new job proved a disaster, and within a year I had moved back home. One of the saving graces of the experience was that I no longer took for granted the things I had thought I was tired of; after my year in exile, they seemed new and fresh. I knew the place in a different way than I had known it before.

When you walk today, think of your route as an exploration and return. There is a reason why circles are a universal motif: They symbolize completion and fulfillment. Make a loop in your walk, coming back by a different route than your outbound path. Whether you walk around a pond or a series of city blocks, make it a metaphor for the change that occurs in you as you walk. The point is not that when you finish, you're back where you started. It's that you're back to the same point with a different perspective.

As this book closes its own loop, I hope you've gotten some ideas for new ways to use and enjoy your walks—and that you start today to expect one special thing to come from each excursion. Whether you MindWalk to take a break from your day, to get in closer touch with yourself or the world around you, or simply to pass the time while getting from here to there doesn't matter; it's your attitude that counts. I'd love to hear from you about the joys you find and how you find them. Together, we can help inspire one another and make our lives a little richer every day. Here's to walking—from the neck up!

Write to:
MindWalks
P.O. Box 382346-B
Cambridge, MA 02238
mfrakes@mindwalks.com
www.mindwalks.com

Walking Techniques and Tips

Walking provides physical as well as mental benefits. Here are some tips on proper walking form that can help make your walk more of a workout:

Feet. When you step, roll squarely from heel to toe; don't let the foot roll toward either side. Push off with the ball of your back foot. Keep your feet parallel.

Legs. If you want to move faster, take more steps per minute while maintaining your natural stride length.

Hips. Tuck your pelvis slightly (think of trying to touch your spine with your belly button). As you step, extend the leg from the hip, letting your pelvis rotate forward with each leg. This allows you to cover more ground without bouncing.

Stomach. Keep your abdominal muscles firm enough that they automatically make you stand up straighter, but not so tight that they interfere with breathing.

Arms. Bend your arms. Speed walkers keep them at a right angle, but even a wider angle gives you more power; it also helps prevent swelling caused by gravity drawing fluid into your hands. Let your arms swing back and forth from your shoulders like pendulums swinging in parallel lines; don't bring them across your body. Drop your shoulders.

Head. Keep it level and balanced above your shoulders.

Additional Resources

Here are some resources that can help you develop a formal walking exercise program:

Prevention's Practical Encyclopedia of Walking for Health: From Age-Reversal to Weight Loss, the Most Complete Guide Ever by Mark Bricklin and Maggie Spilner. This comprehensive guide from editors at *Prevention* magazine is out of print, but it's worth searching for. Some of the information could use updating, but it takes a common-sense approach to a wide variety of walking topics, including scientific research on the benefits of walking and personal tips from *Prevention* readers.

Walking Medicine: The Lifetime Guide to Preventive and Rehabilitative Exercise-walking Programs by Gary Yanker and Kathy Burton (McGraw-Hill, 1990). Prescribes walking regimens for a variety of medical situations, including cardiovascular problems and respiratory conditions.

The 90-Day Fitness Walking Program by Mark Fenton and Seth Bauer (Perigee, 1995). Suggests a step-by-step regimen to introduce novices to walking for exercise.

The Healthy Heart Walking Book: The American Heart Association Walking Program by the American Heart Association (Macmillan General Reference, 1995). Suggests a simple walking program and includes a walking diary for recording progress.

Walking: A Complete Guide to the Complete Exercise by Casey Meyers (Random House, 1992). Includes nutritional tips and helpful diagrams to demonstrate proper walking form.

Fitness Walking: Technique, Motivation, and 60 Workouts for Walkers by Therese Iknoian (Human Kinetics Publishing, 1995). Focuses on charts that spell out detailed regimens for a variety of fitness levels and workout times.

Walk Aerobics by Les Snowdon and Maggie Humphreys (Penguin USA, 1996). Discusses benefits of walking as both exercise and stress reliever.

Prevention magazine, which covers health and fitness, has a monthly "Walking Fit" column. It sponsors the *Prevention* Walking Club; membership includes six issues of the club's newsletter and a log to track your progress. The magazine also has a web site found at (www.healthyideas.com).

Walking magazine comes out six times a year. In addition to articles on walking, fitness and nutrition, it also reviews new walking shoes twice annually.

American Volkssport Association (AVA), which has chapters in many U.S. cities, sponsors noncompetitive walking events and designated trails; these outings are designed for a range of fitness levels. Members track their walks and distances to receive awards. Volkssport began in Europe, and the AVA is affiliated with the International Federation of Popular Sports. Address: 1001 Pat Booker Rd., Suite 101, Universal City, TX 78148.

Phone: (800) 830-WALK for information about membership or to listen to a prerecorded list of upcoming events across the U.S. Web address: www.ava.org.

The web site called Wendy's Walking Page includes articles and a comprehensive set of links to other walking-related sites. You also can sign up to get e-mailed messages from other walkers. The address is http://walking.tqn.com/mbody.htm.

If you're interested in ecopsychology, Dr. Michael Cohen's web site offers his book, *Reconnecting with Nature*, as well as some samples of an educational program that demonstrates the importance of staying in touch with the natural world. Web address: http://www.pacificrim.net/~nature.

Many charitable organizations sponsor fund-raising walks. Check with the local chapter of such groups as the American Heart Association, the American Diabetes Association, and the American Cancer Association to find out about walks in your area.

Stay in Touch!

Join the MindWalks revolution! Start a MindWalks group of your own; just write or e-mail me at the address below for free information that can help get you started. Or join us on one of our upcoming MindWalks tours.

And I'd love to hear about your own MindWalks. What discoveries have you made that inspired you? What do you do on your walks to help you get unstuck on a mental challenge or to manage your emotions? What do you think about when you're walking that helps keep you going when the going gets tough?

Contact me at:

> MindWalks
> P.O. Box 382346-B
> Cambridge, MA 02238
>
> www.mindwalks.com
>
> mfrakes@mindwalks.com

Thanks for becoming a MindWalker!

MindWalks Products

MindWalks
- The book that helps you enjoy the mental benefits of walking
- Pocket-sized for convenience

MindWalks with Music (available Spring 1999)
- Audio MindWalks created just for this tape!
- Individual segments let you control how long you walk
- 40-minute tape helps pick up your pace or soothe your spirit. You decide!

MindWalks book and tape combination package (available Spring 1999)
- Discounted package makes a great gift! (Free gift wrap included.)

My MindWalks Journal (available Spring 1999)
- For recording the special things you experience on your own MindWalks.
- Includes quotes that inspire you to reach your goals.

MindWalks workshops and retreats (available Fall 1999; contact us for information)

For free information on starting a MindWalks™ group of your own, fill out the form at the end of this book, or contact:

> MindWalks
> P.O. Box 382346-B
> Cambridge, MA 02238
> 1 (877) MINDWALK (toll-free)
>
> www.mindwalks.com
>
> mfrakes@mindwalks.com